Selima Hill grew up in a family of painters on farms in England and Wales, and has lived by the sea in Dorset for over 40 years. She was awarded the King's Gold Medal for Poetry 2022 with special recognition for *Gloria: Selected Poems* (Bloodaxe Books, 2008). She received a Cholmondeley Award in 1986, and was a Royal Literary Fund Fellow at Exeter University in 2003-06.

She won first prize in the Arvon/*Observer* International Poetry Competition with part of *The Accumulation of Small Acts of Kindness* (1989), one of several extended sequences in *Gloria* (2008). *Gloria* also includes work from *Saying Hello at the Station* (1984), *My Darling Camel* (1988), *A Little Book of Meat* (1993), *Aeroplanes of the World* (1994), *Violet* (1997), *Bunny* (2001), *Portrait of My Lover as a Horse* (2002), *Lou-Lou* (2004) and *Red Roses* (2006).

Her later collections from Bloodaxe are: *The Hat* (2008); *Fruitcake* (2009); *People Who Like Meatballs* (2012), shortlisted for both the Forward Poetry Prize and the Costa Poetry Award; *The Sparkling Jewel of Naturism* (2014); *Jutland* (2015), shortlisted for both the T.S. Eliot Prize and the Roehampton Poetry Prize; *The Magnitude of My Sublime Existence* (2016), shortlisted for the Roehampton Poetry Prize; *Splash Like Jesus* (2017); *I May Be Stupid But I'm Not That Stupid* (2019); *Men Who Feed Pigeons* (2021), shortlisted for the 2021 T.S. Eliot Prize and 2021 Forward Prize and for the 2022 Rathbones Folio Prize; and *Women in Comfortable Shoes* (2023).

Violet was a Poetry Book Society Choice and was shortlisted for all three of the UK's major poetry prizes, the Forward Prize, T.S. Eliot Prize and Whitbread Poetry Award. *Bunny* won the Whitbread Poetry Award, was a Poetry Book Society Choice, and was shortlisted for the T.S. Eliot Prize. *Lou-Lou* and *The Hat* were Poetry Book Society Recommendations, as is *Women in Comfortable Shoes*, while *Jutland* was a Special Commendation.

SELIMA HILL

Women in
Comfortable Shoes

BLOODAXE BOOKS

ISBN: 978 1 78037 667 7

First published 2023 by
Bloodaxe Books Ltd,
Eastburn,
South Park,
Hexham,
Northumberland NE46 1BS.

www.bloodaxebooks.com
For further information about Bloodaxe titles
please visit our website and join our mailing list
or write to the above address for a catalogue

Supported using public funding by
**ARTS COUNCIL
ENGLAND**

Cover design: Neil Astley & Pamela Robertson-Pearce.

Printed in Great Britain by Bell & Bain Limited, Glasgow, Scotland, on
acid-free paper sourced from mills with FSC chain of custody certification.

ACKNOWLEDGEMENTS

Acknowledgements are due to the publishers of the following pamphlets were some of these poems first appeared: *Fridge* (The Rialto, 2020), *My Mother with a Beetle in Her Hair* (Shoestring Press, 2020), *Dancing Lessons for the Very Shy* (Guillemot Press, 2023); as well as to Nadia Kingley's Fair Acre Press, publisher of the following eight pamphlets included in a set of twelve entitled *What to Wear in Bed* (2022): *The Chauffeur*; *Dolly*; *Dressed and Sobbing*; *Fishface*; *My Friend Weasel*; *Reduced to a Quivering Jelly;* and *Susan*. Some of the titles and content of the sequences included in these pamphlets have since been revised. Some poems have also appeared in the *London Review of Books*, *Poetry London*, *Poetry North*, *The Poetry Review*, *The Rialto* and *Ver Poets*.

I would like to offer my heartfelt thanks to Neil Astley for his help and encouragement over many years; to Jo and Lorraine, the librarians at my local library; to R.C.H. for the pre-loved A4 envelopes; to the Mitchell family for the delights of Gravel Hill; to Paul the lifeguard (not for saving my life, not yet anyway, but for being ready to save it); and to the indispensable and unrufflable Penny. I would also like to thank Dr Chocolate and Mr Sheep (who are too modest to let me thank them by their other names): they have been invaluable. I would especially like to thank Michelle MacKenzie – so diligent and yet so cheery!

The epigraph by Per Petterson is from *Ut og stjæle hester* (2003) translated by Anne Born as *Out Stealing Horses* (Harvill Secker, 2005).

CONTENTS

Fishface

My Friend Weasel

Susan and Me

Dolly

My Mother with a Beetle in Her Hair

Fridge

My Spanish Swimsuit

The Chauffeur

Women without Hamsters

1 | *Dancing Lessons for the Very Shy*

Reduced to a Quivering Jelly

Dressed and Sobbing

It would all be different if I had owned a horse.

PER PETTERSON

You've finally written it? That's great! She asked me if I'd read to her from it and I said no. Just a paragraph? No. A sentence? No. Half a sentence! One word? No. A letter? I said okay, that I would read the first letter of the novel. She smiled and closed her eyes and sort of burrowed into her bed like she was preparing herself for a delicious treat. I asked her if she was ready and she nodded, still smiling, eyes closed. I stood and cleared my throat and paused and then began to read.

L.

She sighed and lifted her chin to the ceiling, opened her eyes and told me it was beautiful, BEAUTIFUL, and true, the best thing I'd written yet. I thanked her and shoved the page back into the plastic Safeway bag.

MIRIAM TOEWS: *All My Puny Sorrows* (2014)

My Mother with a Pair of Scissors

Why's my mother never seen at school?
Or even in the neighbour's house next door?

Is she fast asleep in her eye-mask?
Or does she creep around the house with scissors

looking for a wing to be clipped?
Does she cower, drenched in eucalyptus oil,

in bedding primed with orange peel and Marmite,
listening for the whine of the mosquitoes

who track her day and night, who won't let go,
who aren't so much devoted as deranged?

Whatever is she doing all the time
alone in our enormous house next door?

Is she frightened? I have no idea.
Maybe she just sleeps all day like pears.

The Green Bear

The house my mother lives in is not suitable
for little girls and so I'm living here.

Here I am allowed to have a dog.
The dog is large and sad like a sandbag.

Once a nurse gave me a bear.
The bear was thin and green. I never liked it.

Ponies

The nostrils of the man whose house I'm living in
sprout gigantic toffee-coloured whiskers.
I see them when he steps into his car.
That's all I know. Then he disappears.
And yet he is her own beloved husband.
She draws him pretty pictures of ponies
he chucks into the bin on his way out.

The Boiled Egg

I'm sitting in her bathroom in her nightie
watching her powder her nose.
I'm here to be her guest, her welcome guest,
while everybody else is somewhere else.

We give the Labrador his morning tea.
His bottom and his nose are pale brown
like nylon stockings only rubbery.
She boils me an egg. I think *chick*.

Good Morning, Reverend Mother

I want to whisper What's the matter, Mother?
Weren't you once a normal girl like me?

I want to but I don't. I bend my knee
and say, in tears, *Good morning, Reverend Mother.*

Wasps

Lying on my back in the dark,
I'm floating like a jelly being set.

Nothing is allowed to disturb me.
Hands and lips are chased away like wasps.

Real Cherries

She's standing by the cooker in the sun
watching me nibble stale cake.

I'm digging out the bits of glacé cherry
and asking God to lead me to a big one.

Of course I know they're not real cherries.
Did they live? The answer is no.

Edith

As everybody knows, she knows nothing –
but everybody's wrong. She knows a lot.

How to tango, how to please cats,
when to talk to strangers, when to laugh,

and whether it's a good idea or not
to be alone upstairs with Tunnock's Tea Cakes.

The Blessed Virgin Mary's Ears

She hears my prayers with her secret ears.
She hears them but she doesn't want to answer.

And why's she always got up so impractically?
No wonder she looks charming but pissed off.

Melted Chocolate

I've made a little fire in the ashtray
and feed it with a picture of Mary.
(It's only a picture after all.)
It singes her unfashionable dress
and warms the alabaster of the ashtray
where somebody has carved the word CORNWALL
('carved'? 'engraved'?) – somebody unknown
who may or may not be a pyromaniac,
who may or may not tiptoe to a cliff-top

with keys to someone's cottage and some paraffin
and start a fire that will blaze all night;
and crowds will gather, questions will be asked,
and he – the pyromaniac – will watch
from where he's bobbing in a stolen boat
now stocked with everything he's going to need...
I prod the little fire with my fork.
My fingers are as warm as melted chocolate,
as bougainvillea in warm Brazil.

What *Other Things?*

Although it looks like ordinary water
this water's holy, Edith's saying. *Holy.*

I have to make the sign of the cross.
I'm a sinner. Which I really like.

She gives me cupcakes but *the other things*
she's keeping from me for my own good.

Mother Mary

Mother Mary's not a real mother.
She isn't even really a woman.

She isn't even human. She scuttles;
she hides in holes; she thinks she'll soon be eaten.

Mountaineering

On the other side of the wall,
in figure-hugging boiler-suit and mittens,
the dentist is tending his begonias
and cursing the malignant little schoolgirl

whose two unruly cherry-red sandals
are dangerously near his greenhouse roof.
Above him, by a window on a balcony,
a giant fan goes round and round and round.

He goes indoors. It's time for his nap.
He'll stretch out on his bed in his underpants
and dream of being lost in the fastnesses
of mountains which aren't mountains but teeth.

People in Taxis

She puts – she *pops* – her finger on my nose –
the 'button nose' that makes me so adorable,
so like a little pug, or pig, or piglet;

she thinks it's just so yummy she could chew it –
as soft as cheeks, as chubby as tomatoes,
as puppy fat that's begging to be nuzzled;

she can't resist feeding me with sugar-lumps
while those who are less fond of *helping others*
glide about the capital in taxis.

What to Wear in Bed

Everything about him is mysterious –
his tiny hat, his ring, his ginger stubble.
I've only ever seen him by his car,
either stepping in or stepping out.
Never in the house or in the garden
or walking down the street like the rest of us.

His only words, the honks of his horn.
He might as well have come from outer space –
his offices, his garages, his pipes,
the way he moves. As if I don't exist.
I'm just a wingless midge in a boater
(albeit an educated midge).

The boater is part of my uniform.
In winter-time I'm told to wear a beret.
I'm told to fast, and when to say my prayers,
and who to pray to, what to wear in bed.
(Every night I'm told that I'm a sinner
and I must wear what sinners wear in bed.)

My Mother on the Verge of Tears

My mother, on the verge of tears as usual,
walks about her house with a tea-towel
twisted round her head like a turban.
Part of her war against mosquitoes.

Can't they understand that she's exhausted
and hasn't got the energy to scratch?
Can't they go and torture someone younger
or, better still, go and *eat grass*?

(Actually she doesn't call it 'tea-towel'.
She calls it 'drying-up cloth' which is longer
and doesn't sound so cosy. But she's like that.
She does not like things to be 'cosy'.)

Lambs

Everybody tells me repeatedly
not to talk to strangers – but I do!
I talk to strangers all the time! I love it!

I ask them what the time is and they stop
and look at me with a loving look
like Jesus with His armfuls of lambs.

Clocks

Being horizontal's easy. Clocks
are ticking on the walls and on the tables.

I can have whatever I want.
Even the Bulgarian kaleidoscope.

She says she was *unhappy in love*.
She sits beside the bed. *He was a priest*.

Who? I ask. *Who was a priest?*
But all she does is tap me on the nose.

I ask her if the doctor will be nice.
She taps me like an egg and says *He'd better be*.

(And as for being saved, I'll save myself.
The Virgin Mary looks too bored to bother.)

The Man in the Veil

If I climb on top of the wall
I can see, or glimpse, another world
where tiny figures steer enormous wheelbarrows

and, if I wait, the man in the veil,
who gives me funny waves as if he's hoping
I'm absolutely terrified of bees.

I smile at the man as if to say:
Terrified? I *love* being stung!

The Toot of the Jag

I'm perched on what she calls the banquette
eating food we never had at home –
custard creams, custard tarts, meringue shells –
and glasses of fluorescent orange squash.

After tea I write to the Queen,
draw an owl and sprinkle it with glitter.
And when I hear the toot of the Jag
I fly upstairs as fast as I can.

The Word *Laburnum*

At first I didn't know what they meant.
I didn't know that what they meant was: *poison*.

But why obey when you can disobey?
I suck the pods I'm not allowed to suck

and feel something I'm too proud to fear
the word *laburnum* tells me I'm enjoying.

Rounders

I whack the rock-hard ball and run like hell
and pray to God to *grant me the audacity*
to give it such a whack it clears the wall

and hits a sinner *smack* on the head.
Sister Winifred looks bored stiff.
Typical. Athleticism stinks.

Ants

They march across the floor like bougainvillea –
orange, gold, vermilion and dumb.

The grains of sugar glitter on the mat.
She plucks a hair – a whisker – from her chin

with tweezers I've been using for the liver
I feed the tadpoles in the salad bowl.

This Nasty Chair

While everybody else proceeds straight in
I have to sit outside. This nasty chair
has been set up outside just for me.

Nothing moves except the occasional nun
who shuffles past without looking up.
(Once a nun came up to me and *bit me*.

She bit me on the jaw. You don't believe me?
Very well then, don't. But she did.)
Everybody's fasting except me.

Switzerland

Downstairs in the kitchen, on the landing,
clocks are ticking, time is passing. Cuckoos

cuckoo in the dark in rustic Swiss
as if they haven't realised I can't ski.

Fishface

I thought I liked the cat but I don't.
And he – the cat – doesn't like me.
He doesn't like anything but fish
and sicking up the fish in the basket
the patient dog tries in vain to sleep in.
All she wants to do is sleep and sleep!

(In that way the dog is like my mother.
She would sleep for ever if she could –
to get away from thinking about me,
me and my big smile, she can't stand it,
it follows her around as she paces
from room to room, armed with citronella.)

Zvuv

Half-naked in her ankle-length dressing-gown,
my mother is battling with mosquitoes –

or not so much battling with as bowing to –
the phalanxes of bloodthirsty mosquitoes

that whine their high-pitched whines in her hair
and will not let her sleep. *Not a chance.*

Mosquitoes have got too many legs.
They've come to give her elephantiasis.

They like to breed in buckets. They say *zvav*.
They think that what they say explains everything.

Notes

The word 'cosy' ('My Mother on the Verge of Tears') always makes me think of Alex ('Free-Solo') Honnold in *Alone on the Wall*: 'Nobody achieves anything because they're happy and cosy.' I'm not saying I agree, by the way.

Bougainvillea ('Melted Chocolate', 'Ants') is a shrub named after the French navigator, Bougainville. Laburnum is a tree with yellow pendulous racemes and poisonous pods. I don't know where the word 'laburnum' comes from but I like it.

Fishface ('The Cat') is one of the names given to a character in a book for children by Edward Ardizzone. Here it is the name of a cat.

Zvuv is the Hebrew word for mosquito. It means Lord of the Flies, I've been told. Mosquito means little fly (and not little mosque).

MY FRIEND WEASEL

Perfection

All we want to do is spend our days
walking upside down on our hands
across the lawn and round the lily pond.
We brush the daisies with our perfect hair.
Everything about us is perfect –
our Aertex shirts, our Chilprufe underwear,
our tiny shorts the colour of meringues.

The Plait

She comes to school in a limousine,
alone, afraid, driven by a chauffeur
we'll realise only later is her father.
A plait hangs down her back like a weasel
hanging in a wood from a post.

The New Assistant Matron

Every night the new assistant matron
reads aloud to us and every night
we ride our little ponies till we reach,
we dream we reach, the end of the world.

Flamingos

Our mothers send us letters we don't read –
or if we do we don't admit we do.
And some of us get parcels from them too –
peanut butter, fudge, a squashed tartine
we eat with teaspoons on each other's beds
and talk about our ponies and our guinea pigs
and some of us, lying through our teeth,
talk about the fathers we've invented –
they're young, they're tall, they're kind, they breed flamingos
that let us feed them rehydrated shrimp.

The Daughter of the Chauffeur

My new best friend, the daughter of the chauffeur,
is so incredibly shy she talks to no one
and no one talks to her. Only me.
I talk to her as gently as I can.
Gentleness is something we find easy,
we, the boarders, we, the lost souls,
who talk to teddies, daddy-long-legs, trout,
who talk in code to our pyjama-cases.

My Mother Visits My Father

When she pops her head round his door
it's like a visit from a mother hen
he either takes no notice of at all
or shoos back out into her run again.
I don't know how she can. I'd rather die
than pop my little head round the door
that polymaths and polyglots with books
the size and shape of tombstones pour through,
with books and cakes and striped and spotted flowers
sprayed with heady perfume and insecticide.

Gravel in Our Hair

Upside down, together and invincible,
with gravel in our elbows and our hair,
we never stop perfecting our somersaults
because we know how good perfection feels.

The Pilot

The new girl says her father was a pilot
who thinks he's flown to Heaven by mistake.
He sits indoors like an iced cake
and doesn't know how frightening he is.

Those Who Love Their Fathers

We lock our five-year diaries in our lockers,
we hide the cards, we hide the photographs,
we hide the brown rectangular packages
that nobody must know that the fathers
of those who love their fathers duly send.

The Queen

Her father is a doctor. And, she says,
he's seen the Queen naked. We're impressed.
We dream of love. Not just any love –
the love of someone naked we don't know.

What We Do After Church

After church we gather in the cedar tree.
This is where we spend our free time,
sitting down or walking about.
Far away our mothers and our fathers
think we love them and perhaps we do.
Perhaps we do and perhaps we don't.
God is giving nothing away.

One Hot Day

One hot day, the French girl says, her father
walked into a forest in his suit
and late that afternoon they found his body –
a death, she says, which surprised no one.

Tennis

Far below us we can see the lily pond,
the silent cows, the teachers playing tennis.
Everything looks innocent from here,
perfected and incapable of change.

Horses

Why they had children in the first place
they can't remember, or they never knew
but anyhow our fathers are preoccupied,
their houses hushed like houses made of down.
Our mothers, with their handbags and their lipsticks,
existent in the sense that God exists –
benighted, incorruptible and pained –
our mothers are pretending to be mothers
while we ourselves pretend to be horses.

The Shimmering Plains of Africa

We creep along the hedge with our swimming things
and stale doughnuts stolen from the bins
and when at last we reach the secret lake
Matron can be seen neatly parking
her Sunbeam Talbot by the willow trees.
She holds the door open like a chauffeur.
We pile in. The seats are real leather.
Matron, in her Gor-Ray skirt and cardigan,
who combs our hair, who calls us *her giraffes*;
whose hair is like the shimmering plains of Africa,
who gets us out of bed to see the moon;
who lets us smear Nutella on our bacon
and gives the homesick lemon meringue pie;
is capable of nothing except something
we later understand to be love.

Golf

From here it's so high up we can see
the chapel and the stables and the river
and, out beyond the river, the fairway
where giant men play golf with giant sons.

Out of Reach in Their Enormous Coats

They want to understand us but they don't,
they don't, they can't, they become enraged,
they hate our eyes, our undulating hair,
the way we never stop becoming women.
They think we never speak but we do,
we speak to cats, to ponies, to each other,
of course we do, we just don't speak to them,
out of reach in their enormous coats
in which they are reduced to being hands,
pink and fat, like peonies or roses.

Hula-hooping on the Log-shed Roof

No wonder they can't stand it. I mean look at us
hula-hooping on the log-shed roof.
Showing off again. They can't stand it.
We need to think of others for a change.
They tilt their heads. They drop their eye-drops in.
They float away like babies in formaldehyde.

Rabbit Pie

We're here because we're here to be forgotten,
to spare them from the pain of us ungraciously
avoiding them. Their eyes, their smell, their hair.
They keep us here like rabbits in a pie.

Hairbrushes

Now we have forgotten who they are.
We haven't even noticed we've forgotten.
All we notice now is our hair
and which of us has got the most chic hairbrush.

Brigitte Bardot

My timid friend has spent all afternoon
sticking pictures in her secret book
on which two perfect Bs are being drawn.
They touch the book like words of a prayer,
or like a single word, repeated: *please*.

Summer Term

The assistant matron's shimmering eyes and eyelids,
the shimmering tufts of lemon meringue pie,
the shimmering hooks and eyes of tiny bras,
the shimmering Sunbeam Talbot's tortoiseshell dash,
the shimmering courts, the shimmering drool of cows,
the smooth and shimmering marble of our armpits
shimmer in our hearts and souls all summer,
knocking being homesick on the head.

Sherbet Lemons

Perched up in the tree we're not allowed in,
we suck our sherbet lemons – while our fathers
strut around the desks of distant offices
encased in suits like men encased in icicles;
our disinfected mothers, meanwhile,
squeezed inside their corsets, slips and brassieres
take up their positions in their kitchens
while doing all they can not to think
they might become – *already are* – unnecessary.

People at a Cat Show

Do we love our parents? Maybe.
Or maybe it's their absence that we love.
Anyhow neither of us mentions them –
any more than people at a cat show
will ever mention cats with three legs.

Mosquitos

To go beyond the gate is forbidden;
to reach the hidden lake where the mosquitos
can't believe how lovely we are,
how meaty and how warm, is forbidden;
to lie beside the lake in the sun
licking chocolate pennies is forbidden;
to wear forbidden underwear, forbidden;
to question who or what we are, forbidden;
to touch ourselves, to hurt ourselves, forbidden;
to skinny-dip, forbidden; friend, forbidden.

Lights Out

In the semi-darkness of the dormitories
we whisper in the ears of those we love
while in the bedside lockers tiny bras
are waiting for their owners to get used to them.

My Friend's Uncle's Tortoise

She did once say her uncle had a tortoise.
Apart from that she never mentions home.
And as for me, I'm like her bodyguard.
Everybody's got to understand
nobody must touch her. Even me.
And she must always have her own way.

Young Ladies

We do not like the regulation swimsuits
we wrap ourselves in towels to not be seen in.
We do not like how chaste they make us feel.
Or how the driver calls us his *young ladies.*

Rudolf Nureyev's Hair

The doctor's hair is short and white and curly.
He waddles like a curly kind of goose.
We prefer our men to be Russian
and preferably born on a train.

Swimming in the Lake

It feels less like swimming in a lake
than swimming in and out of priceless mirrors
made of silver ice and golden chains.
On the bank my spellbound entourage
is willing me to drown but I refuse.
My brain is like the brains of the dead
who see a light that reveals nothing...
I met my father in the white hotel.
It was winter. Snow lay on the ground.
I wore the woollen pinafore dress
with buttons on I'd sewn on myself.
My father wore an ankle-length coat
that in my mind my father wears for ever.
Today the fathers and the mothers still
walk their daughters here beside the lake
that plays a little game with itself
to see how like a cradle it can creak.

Sunday

The priest is waiting for us on the steps.
He leers at us. We're proud of our disdain.
Can't he understand we are perfect?
And if we sin our sins are perfect too?

Mothers, Mothers, Mothers

They pull on their expensive nylon stockings
and take up their positions at the sinks
of kitchens as irrelevant as kitchen shops
where nothing is alive except flies.

Candelabra

My silent friend gets weaker and weaker,
her head's too weak to hold up her hair,
and every time she goes to see the doctor
the matron says I have to go in with her
and talk about her cat, Candelabra,
and Candelabra's home, Uzbekistan.

Summer

On summer days we gather in the cedar tree,
squeezing splinters and comparing breasts;
we gather in the dusk and sniff the dark
and watch ourselves grow older and older.

Violets

People who aren't shy think those who are
need to be *shouted at* but shouting
makes the people who aren't shy so hoarse
they kick the people who are shy instead
or, if there's room, shut them in a cupboard.

Fleas

Our fathers send us here to be trained.
We're being trained like fleas to obey.
We're being trained again and again.
Some, however, learn to disobey.

Marriage

The fact our mothers married our fathers
is something we don't ever want to think about –
it's easier to think they're rubber parents
of rubber children in a rubber world.
Everybody trusts them. They're so charming.
We, however, only trust ourselves.
We sit in rows like wolves in the cedar tree
and wait together for our hearts to break.

Mouse

It's midnight in the dormitory. Our lips
are softer than the softest lipless moths
as in our dreams they settle on the horses
that nuzzle our elasticated boots.
My friend's awake. She wants to disappear.
Her body wants to disappear too.
She doesn't eat. She doesn't menstruate.
Her breath is like the whisker of a mouse.

End-of-term Concert

Our parents sit in rows like small children.
We ourselves stand about like storks –
the violinists with their violins,
the clarinettists with their clarinets
and me, with straightened hair, with the oboe
I never want to have to play again.
A pale count presents me with a cup.
He's telling me to *follow my dream*.
I did, I did. I dreamt I was a flower
circling round the surface of a swimming-pool
with nothing else to do but fall apart.

Train

End of term. Journey to the station.
Men we bait treating us like meat.
Everybody in the carriage thinking
these are very dirty little girls.

Toilets, Waterloo Station

We roll our grubby skirts up really short,
we rip our shirts, we back-comb our hair,
we smoke, we drink, we swear, we do our best
to re-emerge as people people shun.
We smell of cigarettes and patchouli.
We start to sing and fall about laughing,
or anyway we all fall about,
I don't know if we're laughing or crying.

Uzbekistan

Uzbekistan is Candelabra's homeland.
Candelabra is my friend's cat.
Is or was. It must be dead by now.
My dead-cat friend probably is too.
I mean she got as thin as a fly
and isn't worth bothering about.

The House

Because he likes to hear the pigeons coo,
my father's room is right at the top.
My mother's room is here, next to mine.
Apparently I'm *going off the rails.*
I dress in stolen flowers and stolen necklaces
and, thus arrayed, am *going off the rails.*
Children's home, detention centre, Borstal,
they threaten me with everything they can.
Idiots. They're wasting their time.
I never listen to a word they say.
The only thing I listen to's the planets'
elliptical unsyncopated whoosh.

Love is the difficult realisation that something other than oneself is real.

IRIS MURDOCH

The New Girl

There seemed to be no reason we were friends.
But anyhow why talk about reasons?

She was just a normal happy new girl.
It was only later that she wasn't.

Her Bedside Locker

Like the locker that was such a mess
the matrons had no choice but to devise

punishments they told themselves were reasonable,
her peeling body made their hearts sink.

The Horse

Outside the smallest house I'd ever been inside
(far less slept in, squeezed against the ceiling

between her growly dog and her mother,
who lay awake, too afraid to move)

stood a massive horse attracting flies
the way a swollen breast attracts a mouth.

Her Late Mother's *Mason Pearson* Hairbrush

Thwarted and forgotten, she survived
by rhythmically brushing her hair

and modelling me anything I asked for –
a pony, a matron – out of mud.

Like Painted Barges

Like painted barges being weighed down
by dreams of love we couldn't understand,

like heavy barges peeling in the heat,
all we ever did was exhaust ourselves.

Without Sin

It was either chaste or naïve,
or something in between, or something else –

the friendship of a sack for a sack
when no one knows or cares what they contain.

Other friendships were considered sinful
but there was nothing sinful about ours.

A Man with a Palm

We lived without caresses. Unlike me,
she would, and did, submit to anything.

She studied Ancient Greek. She gave up butter.
Let herself be bullied and enslaved.

And every day she grew. She grew so tall
she wasn't like a person any more

and talking to her was a waste of time.
As for me, I'd had this revelation

that matrons and their discipline meant nothing,
absolutely nothing, and my time,

day and night, was now taken up
with concentrating on my disobedience.

I nursed it like a man with a palm.
I worshipped it. I was in love with it.

The Love of One Potato for Another

Our love was like the love of two potatoes
by which I mean it wasn't love – potatoes

come in lots of different shapes and sizes
but none of them is capable of love.

We were only capable of waiting –
in which, alone, misled, we luxuriated.

The Blood-stained Mower

With drawings of our ponies, of our underwear,
of those we took delight in being mean about

and those we fell in love with – like the gardener
whose dusty, blood-stained boiler-suit we marvelled at

and at the boots and at the blood-stained mower
we lay and sunbathed naked to the sound of

(OK, I may be wrong about the blood-stains) –
we wrote our journals till our hands were raw.

Disobedience

Since I had discovered disobedience
I didn't need, as she did, to affect

elegance, or modesty. I spat at
the matrons and their withered private parts.

Her Green-and-white-striped Dress

Her green-and-white-striped dress, the same as mine –
the sort of dress you'd wear to ride a goat

or murder someone on a dark night –
was not entirely clean, and much too tight,

but, unlike me, she didn't take it off
to mark the hottest day of the year

by lying naked in the long grass
waiting for the man who rode the mower.

The Lesson

She read the lesson not with joy, it's true,
but with a kind of awe-struck intelligence,

looking gravely down at the verses
like someone in a boat might look down

at headless creatures on the seabed
who steadfastly refuse to be normal.

Sailing

When we reached the boathouse, it was hot
and I refused to move. The next day

we rode from one parched valley to another
on someone else's ponies, bored to tears.

Acne

I'd sometimes catch her picking at her cheek,
as if she'd like to swap it for a mouse's;

as if she knew that people who are tall
are tall because they need to die unaided.

Flapjacks

Whenever we were bored we made flapjacks
and played slow games of cards like old men,

establishing a sort of half-hearted
but nevertheless companionable rhythm.

Pig

I used to take her swimming to the gravel-pits
or, rather, I would swim and she would wallow,

half-submerged like a long pig
that doesn't even grunt or dream of grunting.

Her Father's Car

Sunburnt, in a mini-skirt, with suitcases,
she hid herself underneath a blanket

so nobody would know that the car
making funny noises was her father's.

The Art Galleries and Churches of Central Europe

We spent the whole two weeks being sick.
We didn't have the energy to argue.

In fact we never argued. Like a carp
growing old inside its glassy corridor

where nobody and nothing can disturb it,
she never questioned anything I said

or anything I did. She would smile
and carry on staring at the wall

like a carp that needs all its energy
for eating air and holding back the tears.

Her Little Suitcases

She didn't seem to know how to breathe.
No wonder she was wishing she was dead.

Perhaps she didn't need a friend. I mean
perhaps I somehow stood in her way.

Anyhow we dragged her little suitcases
up and down the hospitals of Europe

side by side and everywhere we went
she peered around at the flood-lit world

like someone who was disappointed in it,
someone who had nothing more to say.

Along the Fringes of This Dazzling World

Along the fringes of this dazzling world
in which I revelled I could see her tiptoe

(if people with enormous feet *can* tiptoe)
or, if not her, I would see her shadow.

Why was I her friend? I've no idea
but in the end I was no use to her.

Bedsit

The tiny room behind the signal box
must have been the last room she was sane in –

if being sane means eating buttered toast
and writing endless stories about signal boxes,

some of which were sheltered in by ponies
whose manes and tails trailed on the ground

and spelt, if you looked hard enough, His name.
The coal-black trains would thunder past and deafen you

and after dark they'd plunge into the stairwell
and up the stairs and tear off all your clothes.

Solid as a Rock

I want to have been *solid as a rock*.
I want to have been able to withstand

hearing what I'd rather not hear,
touching what I'd rather not touch;

I want to have been able to shoulder
someone else's problems as my own –

but even as she told me I was kind
I knew and know I wasn't kind enough.

Curd

When I see her in the threadbare dressing-gown
somebody has wrapped her in like curd,

the gentle face that wishes it was air
now pressed against the wall, I lose my nerve

and walk away in tears, having witnessed
something I am not prepared to bear.

Tinned Fish

They ring me up to tell me she's been found
sitting in a tunnel eating fish.

It doesn't seem to make any sense.
They say it one last time: she is *violent*.

DOLLY

When I Was a Girl I Was Adorable

When I was a girl I was adorable
and all the women who surrounded me

and told me what to do
and what not to do

had also been adorable, we all had,
as sinless and adorable as ducks;

I didn't know it then but even mothers
toddled once, and the fat ones waddled.

Mother Mary

I myself was an angel once.
They sprayed me with gold paint like a car.

Only later would I learn that nuns,
whose pockets rang with rosaries and whistles,

to whom I curtsied, daily, as arranged,
were women, like my mother, in disguise.

On summer afternoons they could be heard
screaming at the little knock-kneed fielders.

Sometimes Mother Mary got the bat
and whacked the ball so hard it hit the wall.

Did our parents visit us? Never.
No one came and went along the passages

except the nuns who lived behind closed doors
polishing their shoes and sucking chicken-bones.

Olivia on the Coach

Squeezed into her tightly-fitting sandals,
she stared at me in such a way I knew

that she and I were enemies (although
neither of us knew what they were).

Mrs Potter the Cook

Her husband was a man of few words
who had a whole annexe to himself

in which he sat admiring his moustache
and making me the pipe-cleaner terriers

she told me we must always refer to
not as simply 'terriers' but as *Bedlingtons*.

Georgina's Mother

Maybe she was jealous, we don't know,
but when she combed her daughters' waist-length hair

she screamed at them so much they were terrified,
I think she even terrified herself,

she screamed at them as if she couldn't stop,
as if her screams would carry on for ever,

as if her screams, long after having killed her,
would carry on screaming for ever.

My Friend Eva

We used to play Halma in her room –
Eva, me and a large bear

she said had lost his wife on the boat.
When we were at school she said he longed for us.

His name was Fritz. His favourite food was sausage.
When we ran back in after school

the house was dark, you couldn't see a thing,
and wedged into the kitchen sat her mother

who never moved from her leather chair.
Her glasses made her eyes look like sweets.

She looked me up and down but didn't speak.
Apparently she didn't speak English.

Although I went there every day for years
I never saw her father but I'd hear

the chirrupings of tiny birds whose feathers
brushed against his shoes in the hall.

And it was here in this gloomy hall
I had my first experience of helping someone.

Lucinda in the Wood

Although I got to school feeling sick
and smelling of the driver's tobacco,

I was there ready with the flask
the billionaire's daughter would be waiting for.

Great-Aunt T.

The richest and by far the oldest woman
I ever knew was the great-great-aunt

I used to visit once a month on Sundays –
a woman like a doll on a bed

that overlooked a lake, or large pond,
said to be the home of an eel.

I envied it its life of simple darkness,
the eyes and lips that slithered round its head...

When my aunt passed away, her cook,
standing by the bed in floods of tears,

handed me a box of chocolate soldiers
lying on their backs beside their guns.

Miss Gee, Matron

Something must have gone very wrong
to find oneself alone with fifty girls –

alone but for the breasts she liked to tuck
inside a singlet last thing at night.

Bernadette Upstairs

She didn't even own her own pony,
her face was like a face made of sleet

and she was cruel, she was like God,
the way He never tells us where the party is.

Doctor Kay

Never be alone with a kitten
and never be alone with a cake

and never be alone with a doctor
because a doctor likes to see you cry,

she likes to hear the sound of small children
suddenly bursting into tears.

Mrs Lawrence, Landlady

She watched me as I ate and as she watched
she smoked the cigarettes that would kill her –

not only her but also the parrot
gasping in the corner of its cage,

its feathers still as blue as the Heavens
waiting for their souls beyond the sky.

Her apron made her look like a man
who thinks it makes him look like a woman.

She kept her cigarettes in the bib,
along with a mouth-freshening spray.

Sophia, Prefect

What I hated most were the clips
that lived and died in hundreds in her hair,

cascades of coloured clips with floral legs
incapable of understanding anything.

Cousin Helen

She picked me flowers and made me apple pies
and cleaned my little kitchen till it glittered

like a kitchen made of snow and ice
and told me what to do and what not to do

as if she were not only my cousin
but a cross between a cousin and a policewoman.

Miss de Vos, Headmistress

She used to give me milk and stale biscuits.
I hated milk. I hated stale biscuits.

And such a heavy chain round her neck
as if she were a ship or a bull.

And eyes so cold they glared like flooded quarries
only the hardiest swimmers can survive,

crack-lipped swimmers who have long forgotten
how to speak or even what their names were.

Marta My Room-mate

Her clothes, her hair, her ears, her little shoulder-bag,
even the letters she sent to her Latvian grandmother,

even the soles of her boots were squeaky clean,
everything was clean except kissing.

Kitty in Term Time

Her hair was like a hood or a veil
as if she couldn't bear to be seen –

not even, by the time she left, by me,
her closest and perhaps her only friend:

I'd spring to her defence like a tigress
famous for its dazzling white teeth.

The Woman on the Mountain

The woman on the mountain was the first
of many women who – and this upsets me –

I must have frightened without meaning to
for reasons I'm still trying to understand.

Mrs A., Abandoned

She baked him special cakes twice a week.
No wonder she was fat! When he left

she watched him out of sight and the crunch
of rubber tread on gravel *did her in*.

Carlotta, the Pianist

With a little kick, she re-arranged
the crimson dress that rippled at her feet.

The piano stood before her like a bay
awaiting the arrival of its swimmers.

Lizzie, Widow

After going nuts at the funeral,
she bought herself a swimsuit and a lake

and started swimming – nervously, at first,
but gradually with what we called *voluptuousness*

until she swam even in the snow,
right across the lake to the island,

and people thought she didn't want to talk to us
but maybe she no longer knew how.

Jean, Out-patient

Holding out her bony arms – like Beanie
holding out her arms towards the keeper

who is and always will be committed,
as long as she is needed, day and night,

to being little Beanie's lost mother –
she staggers round the corner to the Gents.

My Friend Annie

Meeting Annie for the first time
felt like feeling what a pig might feel

shuffling down an alley late one night,
alone and lost and looking for a home,

a ginger pig, now twitching in the moonlight,
who's dreaming of a snout full of root,

whose skin is cracked, whose hairs are dry and bristly,
whose tiny eyes are hidden under ears

like newborn babies hidden in their prams;
whose belly is a meeting-place for worms;

whose knees, if you can call them knees, are wrinkly;
whose purity of heart is like a lettuce;

who doesn't even speak its own language,
after all, this honkless, gruntless pig

has never met another pig before –
and meeting one for the first time.

Edna in the Loo

She sits alone in her little flat
wondering what's happened to her money

like a fish alone in a tank
wondering what's happened to the sea.

Penny in the Opposite Bed

She was being fed through a tube.
Her parents didn't visit any more.

She shivered like a child made of pins
and pins don't ask or even answer questions:

they need to concentrate on overruling
their tiny pointed toes, their glass heads.

Billie My Rival

She hung around the pool in yellow shorts
turning up her little sunburnt nose

at those who couldn't swim and didn't know
that it was cool not to be a lifeguard.

Angelina, My Tutor

Like an orange slug that's wandered off
and lost its slimy way in the snow

where those who search are never seen again
or if they are they can no longer speak,

her orange mouth has sunk into a body
nobody and nothing can make warm again.

Isabel, My New Boss

When I made my way through the moths
to bring her her meringue as if to say

My darling lepidopterist, I love you!
she didn't even bother to look up.

She sat there at her desk with her back to me,
hour after hour, her golden hair

coiled round her head like a snake
her lovers would do anything to finger.

Dr Davey

After lying quietly on her table
for what seemed hours in my underwear,

I felt her hands between my legs like hunters –
intoxicated hunters hunting marmots

who go insane with longing if the marmots,
like God Himself, won't make their presence known.

Linda

Never underestimate the sick,
that's what Dr D always says;

and never underestimate a duck –
the duck of my late uncle, for example,

who lived a life of leisure in his bathroom
simply by her having once been cute.

MY MOTHER WITH A BEETLE
IN HER HAIR

Owls

Because I had to do my homework first
and even then she only let me swim
for twenty minutes at the very most
I'd wait until my mother was asleep
and tiptoe to the lake
on my own,
barely breathing
in the cold and dark
when nothing can be heard but the owls
who've no idea how lucky they are.

My Uncle the Doctor

On very rare occasions
my uncle
would take me to the baths
in a taxi
to teach me how to swim
and use the lockers,
my father was too old
and my mother
would never have set foot in the place
and afterwards,
inside the vast entrance hall,
he'd offer me an evil-looking chocolate,
it was black and tasted of black rot,
of forest floors that never see the light,
but I was much too proud

to spit it out
and anyway I had to be careful,
my uncle was a doctor
and doctors
will operate on girls who are ungrateful,
even those, like me, who could swim,
my tiny head encased in a bathing-cap
dusted by the doctor with the talcum powder
that smelled of what it smells like inside mountains
inhabited by wolverines and moles.

My Mother's Hands

When I was a child I would duck
every time I saw the bony hands
my mother used to gaze at,
full of sorrow,
as if she wished they weren't the hands she touched me with
when – feel them –
she towelled me roughly dry.

The Man with the Tiny Books

The man who sat in what was called the dining-room,
the tyrant who reigned over us like tides,
the man who was no more the man I loved
than men are cows with flowers in the hair,
the man who (but I didn't know it then)
was no less human than the rest of us,
(was made of dust)
he was resolving nothing
by writing, writing in his tiny books
while those of us who dared
would go swimming.

Winter Afternoons at the Pool

I come here every day,
in winter anyway,
and reinvent myself as a fish,
a fish with all the time in the world
to wriggle underwater into history.

My Mother Wearing More Than One Coat

I'm white and wrinkly
but I won't stop swimming
in spite of what my little mother told me,
although to call her *little*'s not polite
but I was like that then,
so impolite,
so inconsiderate and unpredictable
and she was small
and didn't like the water
and felt the cold
even on dry land,
even in her rugs,
in several coats,
she wanted to go home
but I ignored her.

The Pool Attendant at Night

When we've all gone home
he'll lock the doors,
turn the lights out,
take off all his clothes
and slide into the pool like a newt
that thinks it's not a newt but a pool attendant.

The Man Who Looks Like a Baby

There's only me and the man who looks like a baby,
a baby full of milk
with big eyes,
he sits beside the water-cooler, smiling,
and rubs his face,
he can't see a thing,
he lets me be not only me but anyone,
here, like him, to dream,
to not be vertical,
adopting funny shapes like fried eggs.

The Woman from the Nail Bar

The painfully thin woman from the nail bar
(it's horrible to see how thin she is,
as if she wants to disappear,
like down,
as if she isn't worthy of a body)
all she does is work at the nail bar
and after the nail bar starve
and come down here
and crush any lingering hopes
(how dare they linger)
like snails
on the changing-room floor.

Walnut

When my mother died
I think I felt
not so much broken
as whole
like one of those walnuts
on cakes
or Walnut Whips
that anyway *look* whole.

The Girl Who Stroked Cows

Most days I go, or dream of going, swimming
like I used to dream of going,
secretly,
down the muddy land
to stroke the cows,
cows with shit and brambles in their hair,
cows at night with moonlight in their ears,
cows at rest,
cows in pain,
warm cows,
myopic, bony, clueless cows I stroke
because they've got no interest in befriending me,
it's not their thing,
they like to chew and shit,
chew and shit.
(You should see their tails.)

Her One Desire

As I fought my way through the duckweed
that spread across the surface of a lake
the size and shape of something like a concert hall
full of chairs and pianos
made of water
and disappeared between the slimy legs
of sofas made of roots
with mud cushions
inhabited by ancient-looking trout,
my mother would be waving from the bank,
her one desire
to see me wrapped up warmly.

The Stranger on the Bus

A stranger sat beside me on the bus
and asked me what my 'line of work' was,
I said I was retired,
but I'm not,
I work all day, all night, I'm a tailor,
I sew my mother and my father coats,
I sew them coats and hats
to protect them,
not only them,
to protect myself,
stitch by stitch,
we want to be untouched,
we bruise, I tell the stranger, like soft fruit.

Different Kinds of Honey

While the two elaborately-wrinkled women,
should I call them women or ladies,
who look like ballerinas
or ex-ballerinas,
no, I'd better call them ballet-*dancers*,
ballet-*dancers* doesn't sound so girly,
while they stand beside the red NO JUMPING sign
and talk about different kinds of honey,
they totally ignore me,
I'm ignored,
like mashed potato sitting on the plate
of somebody I know
in her wheelchair
repeating in her little piping voice
potato and *potato* and *potato*
but actually I like to be ignored,
to think I look so normal I'm ignorable,
I'm like a sort of spy, I suppose.

My Mother's Daughter

Because I was a difficult child,
violent, morose and inconsolable,
endurance swimming suited me perfectly
but no, my mother called it
showing off,
she had this thing I wanted her attention
although that was the last thing that I wanted,
every breath I took said *go away*,
every little breath,
as, rain or shine,
she sat beside the water underneath
various annoying-looking hats.

The Bony Woman with the Tiny Waist

I have to admit I hope she won't be there,
the bony woman with the tiny waist
who looks about to faint she looks so thin,
and if she does,
crack against the tiles
in nothing but a swimsuit,
just imagine.

My Mother and the Sheep

Once I came downstairs to find a sheep
standing in the kitchen
and my mother
offering the sheep
a ginger biscuit
and looking overjoyed
to have a sheep
suddenly arrive
in her kitchen,
it used to reappear,
I remember,
and fall asleep
in my mother's lap
and keep her nice and warm
while I was swimming.

Looking at Each Other's Breasts in the Changing-room

When to speak the truth was not allowed,
to be undressed,
to look,
was not allowed,
we didn't know we wouldn't mind a bit
how leathery our breasts are
or how few.

My Mother as a Daisy

As I swim serenely up and down
I strip her of the ankle-length mackintosh
she used to sit and wait in on the bank
underneath a pile of old blankets,
and dress her in a tutu
like a daisy
and offer her a corps of smaller daisies
all of whom would rather die
than swim
and sometimes I imagine her on horseback –
somewhere she said girls
should never sit,
never wearing any kind of trouser
and certainly not carrying a whip –
rushing past
cracking a whip.

Café in the Snow

Later I thought
I shouldn't have gone
in the first place,
a snowy day,
as dark as dusk all day,
but I was sick of being stuck indoors
and anyway I like my routine
and I was nearly there,
my yellow bag

bright against the snow,
when I saw it,
a massive cow
hunched against the glass,
it must have skidded on its tiny hooves
and crashed against the solid glass door,
and no one was about,
which was odd,
I peered into the café, I remember,
and saw a swimsuit drying on a hook
and blood,
what looked like blood,
on the tiles,
pools of blood from the wounded cow,
or was I just imagining the cow
the way you do when you're stiff with cold
and think you might have harmed those you love.

The Man with Snow-white Skin

The softly-spoken man with snow-white skin
(even the soles of his feet
are white as snow)
his curly hair a tiny bit longer,
his swimming-trunks a tiny bit tighter
than other people's are,
his round face
as soft and fragrant as a bar of soap,
looks at me like someone in a dream
waving at me
as they fall past.

A Woman with a Bunch of Red Roses

Afterwards I walk the six miles home,
gliding through the snow
like a cat
and meeting not a soul all the way
until I reach the florist's where a woman,
balanced on a pair of kitten heels,
a giant bunch of roses in her arms,
almost knocks me over
as she staggers,
cursing loudly,
out across the snow,
as if to say *why walk when you can totter.*

Having Fun with Babies

Because a group of mothers
in the shallow end
are throwing rosy babies around
like little parcels
in a sorting-office
that only sorts the most exciting parcels,
I pity normal people
on dry land
who don't know what they're missing
and don't want to know.

An Old Man Blue with Cold

An old man,
blue with cold,
in pinstriped swimming-trunks,
lowers himself down
into the pool
where icy ripples
wrap around his knees,
I see him flinch
(I flinched from my mother,
her ring,
where is it now, I wonder,
blue),
down he goes,
backwards,
rung by rung,
and nobody's unkind enough to look,
to say, or to appear to be saying,
he should have given up
years ago.

The Woman with the Plait

Although the sour-faced woman with the plait
reminds me of my sister,
that's not fair,
my sister was a hundred times more miserable,
a thousand times,
and I was merciless,
my mother spent the whole of my childhood
pleading with me in a voice like honey
Can't you just be friends?
but I couldn't,
I'd kneel by my bed and pray to God
to send me down a wasp
or a hornet
so I could watch her dance around the drawing-room
screaming her pretty little head off.

Rabbits

When he drops me off
'in the middle of nowhere',
my lemon-yellow duffle-bag as usual
stuffed with goggles, oranges, the towel
where rows of identical ducks
like identical pilgrims
who know there is something bigger,
if not what,
who walk towards it in enormous boots,
happy to be understanding nothing,

waddle back and forth without a break,
when he drops me off I round the hill
that's always full of rabbits,
rabbits everywhere,
they're on the banks, they're in the lane, they're everywhere,
they've overrun the garden by the shop,
they've colonised the car park
and the climbing-frame
and soon they'll be inside,
at the reception desk,
demanding that they need the pool for weddings.

Friday Night at the Swimming-pool

Because the pool's so empty,
only me,
the silent couple no one knows the name of
and there, in tears, the pot-bellied man
(look away,
even men can cry,
they can and do,
my brother cried once,
teardrops wobbling on his upper lip,
he cried for us,
he cried for his mother,
he cried –
of course, we all do –
for himself)
because the pool's so empty
we can hear
every little heartbreaking sob.

The Man in Purple Swimming-trunks

If the six-foot man in purple swimming-trunks
who thunders up and down like a lorry
crammed with badly-packed chandeliers
would only sit and rest for a while,
maybe have some water from the cooler,
those of us he scatters
could regroup.

The Photograph of My Dog in My Duffle-bag

Why I keep the photo in my duffle-bag
when it makes me sad
I've no idea,
when I feel sadness
like a pelt
brush against the surface of my mind,
ancient,
furtive,
gentle,
like the powder,
my mother's love,
I couldn't bear to touch,
the powder and the flattened powder-puff,
why I keep the photo, I suppose,
is simply to remind me I was loved,
if you can call it love,
that I was shadowed
by a lurcher,
now a lurcher's ghost.

A Very Dark Blue

I go the long way round
because it's snowing,
the sky is blue,
a very dark blue,
the colour of my swimsuit,
almost black,
the colour of the sloes on the mountain,
the lonely little mountain where my mother
wished that I had never been born,
I take the long way home because the snow
is whispering *slow down, my friend,*
slow down.

The Silent Couple No One Really Knows

The silent couple no one really knows,
who never talk,
not even to each other,
who always smile
(but they look so sad!
the man a perfectly useless smiling monk
gliding round a monastery
in slippers,
the wife like dancers
with their broken toes)
the couple people say,
to cheer them up,
you're nearly there to,
are already there.

The Woman in the Salmon-pink Underwear

The man who was 'the man who made me cry'
fed me chocolate kittens in his bed,
I cried because I'd never been so happy,
it was in a bedsit in Romania,
I never say a word about the man,
the tiny vanished world
of his tenderness,
but that's what I am thinking to myself
as side by side we crack our chocolate kittens,
the woman in the salmon-pink underwear
I'm still a bit in awe of, and me.

Delicate Questions from the Young Doctor

He asks me if I think I experience *feelings*,
not thoughts, he's saying, *feelings*,
in my chest,
(he prods me in the chest)
for example
love, he says, I say I don't know,
he asks me if I think I loved my mother
but again I say I don't know
and then I say it's true I rarely cry
and yes, I say, I know I do like swimming
though when I squash my clothes inside the lockers
(and why do lockers have to be so small
with rattly doors
and fiddly little keys)

I feel sadness, yes,
I don't like leaving them,
alone but for a few human hairs,
my clothes, I mean,
still warm from being worn,
I feel sadness,
sorrow,
I don't know,
as if I've got a mouse in my chest
that can't remember what a mouse is for,
that's searching for a god it can believe in,
a feeling in my chest
like at the hospital
in which a heart I know
is slowly beating
while staff adjust and readjust their tubes.

Expensive Swimwear

Unlike us
in our expensive swimwear
my friend is ill,
seriously ill,
I probably won't see her again,
I swim all afternoon,
I swim to nowhere,
to somewhere where she's not too young to die.

No More Potatoes

She wants to feel dead,
not alive,
to never feel anything again,
the nurses give her nothing but potatoes,
please, she whispers,
no more potatoes,
no more mashed potato, no more soup,
no more sodden bedsocks,
no more frocks,
no more yellow copulating crocodiles
made of rubber on the taxi dash,
no more starry nights and shimmering lakes.

FRIDGE

The Beach

The man who dreamt he rode across vast continents
for millions of years
with awestruck followers
famous for their fabulous cuisine,
the swishing of their robes,
their pealing bells,
all of whom have now deserted him,
stares across the sand,
there's no one here,
no one here except two tiny figures,
my mother and myself,
collecting shells.

Rabbits

They sit and smile like contented pies,
they warm my lap,
they tickle my fat cheeks,
they don't know how adorable they are,
adorable and innocent,
like me,
until the day I walk across the moor
and see the hutch,
baking in the sun,
where four enormous rabbits crawl with flies.

Tiny Children

From time to time he'll shudder
like a fridge
where tiny children,
rigid in their sacks,
are being stacked
while crying out for souls.

The Letter

Mothers shouldn't cry
but they do,
my mother cries,
she becomes a stranger,
a stranger other people call my mother,
but no, I will have nothing more to do with her,
no, there's been a terrible mistake,
she's standing in her apron with a letter,
I'm kneeling at the level of her shoe,
and now she walks away towards the compost heap
that's rotting in the sun
attracting snakes.

Other People's Mothers

Other people's mothers are so kind,
they give me biscuits,
sometimes even sweets
wrapped in squeaky paper,
chinking tea-sets,
but if I hear their husbands coming in
I run back home as fast as I can,
home to where my mother
curls upstairs
as if she's been forbidden to come down,
as if she isn't worthy of normality,
as if she has denied herself a life,
alas, my mother is a divorcee,
a divorcee is something like a murderess
but murder I can understand
like jugs.

My Father Dreams He Is a Lorry

The man my mother never called my father
grumbles in his corner like a fridge,
an age-old fridge
dreaming it's a lorry
with secret chambers
nobody can find,
nobody but him
can prise open.

Men with Saws

Carefree,
cool,
I am exempt from pain,
like the man who calls himself Messiah
who always gets to wear his favourite clothes,
gold cravat, gold Birkenstocks, gold watch,
or thought I was,
or tried to be
and longed to be,
until the day I find my friend's mother,
a mother who I knew I could rely on
to be forever cheerful,
wreathed in smiles,
I find my friend's mother at the window
watching men with saws
approach the yew,
and hear the sobs
which lead me to distrust her.

Standing in the Presence of My Father

Standing in the presence of my father,
I feel as uneasy as a child
standing in a field full of fridges
with all the doors torn off
and I can see
bodies,
all exactly the same,
lying on their sides,
with perfect ponytails.

My Father's Roses

While Nellie Moser,
very tall and thin,
spends her days poking through my window
and, taller still, my father's friend The Duchess
whets her thorns
outside the kitchen door,
Lady Luck takes charge of the gate,
of little girls who dare approach the gate,
of girls in shorts with scratches on their knees,
of brazen girls,
of one girl in particular.

My Father's Death

My mother has resigned herself
to being here,
to being gagged,
like me,
to being good,
to being pretty,
but our hearts are cold
and when he dies
they will be colder still,
but when we are alone again
they'll soften
and take up all our time,
these softened hearts.

A Dream of Forgiveness

A beautiful fat pig I call Forgiveness
is standing in my way with a grin
and when I scratch her bristly ears
she grunts
because she knows
nothing else matters.

Kate

Because she is so thin
we are in awe of her,
she moves about the school
like a ghost,
her perfect head
tilted to one side
as if she is too tired to hold it up,
she barely speaks,
any more than grasses,
dried and kept indoors in vases,
speak,
they may have told us
but we weren't listening,
we knew already,
our princess
has won.
Her parents have invited us to visit them
but no,
no way,

not even to the funeral,
to grieve is not the point,
to say we're sorry,
to say she should have just hung on
like they did,
that things would have begun to make sense
is rubbish,
they would never have made sense.

Being Fast Asleep in the Daytime

Being fast asleep in the daytime
suits my mother down to the ground,
sleep is dumb, discreet and non-negotiable,
sleep's the perfect way to be shy.

J.J.

One summer night
he steps onto the bridge,
ties a bunch of roses to the parapet
and jumps into the river
and the water
rolls him to and fro
like gold
in silt.

M.

My face is wreathed in snot,
why didn't God
make me be not me
but a motorway – a motorway
would rather go outside
and choke itself to death on grit
than cry.

My Friend H.

Apparently women never do,
apparently it's only men that *hang themselves*,
girls like us prefer sleeping pills,
of course we've thought of drowning,
slashing wrists,
jumping off a cliff,
express trains,
you've got to get it right,
that's the trouble,
you wouldn't want to end up in some wheelchair
pushed around
by someone you disgust,
it's got to go like clockwork
and be beautiful,
beautiful and effortless –
too late,
she dies
without her knowing it
like roadkill

upside down
in full view of everyone,
born to rule the world
but she didn't,
she ended up in slippers
like the rest of them,
too bored
to even bother to be dead,
too bored to even take the time to kill herself,
someone else had to do that for her,
someone else or *something* else,
whatever,
she had had it up to here,
she was indecent,
she was doomed,
she never got the hang of it,
and now it's time to *grieve*,
and I should know that,
I should and do,
I know so much,
I know
they'll never understand her
or believe her.

Getting Used to It

People die,
they tell me,
so get used to it,
so that's what I am doing,
getting used to it,
though how to do that

no one seems to know,
how to just get used to them,
the suicides
of friends I have encouraged to despair,
OK, not 'encouraged',
I have *witnessed*,
friends I was forbidden to be friends with,
friends who lived in bathrooms, who refused
to meet, to even contact
those who loved them,
friends who never slept,
who *went to pieces*,
friends who didn't answer to their names,
friends in tears,
in blankets,
on their knees,
friends who begged me *not to let them down*.

Babies with Buckets

Who am I forgiving
and for what
and does it really matter,
does it matter
any more than this,
the surgeon's hand,
steadying itself
above a heart;
than here,
in socks,
the babies with their buckets
making grunting noises as they topple.

The Person in the Drawing-room

They tell me I must hurry
but I don't,
I walk sedately down the long street
like someone with a candle on her head,
I reach the house,
a stranger lets me in,
a bed has been set up in the drawing-room,
the stranger brings me coffee in a bowl
and shows me to a chair beside the bed
on which I am transformed
into a person who's not so much a person
as a sack,
a sack the person on the bed is stroked by,
a sack that by some miracle
can run.

The Goose

I've never wished the dead *were still here*,
that anyone who's died would *come back*,
anyone except the goose, perhaps,
the big white goose
who waddled like a fridge,
a fridge with wary eyes on orange legs,
but he was warm
and nothing like a fridge,
imagine trying to cuddle a fridge,
imagine first cuddling
and then *roasting*

a fridge that you have loved,
I don't think so,
so no, I've never sobbed my little heart out
for anyone who's died
except the goose
whose homeless down still floats across the valley
as if to say you'll look but never find him.

How To Be Tidy

My mother, which is typical, is dead,
after all, it's tidy to be dead
and being dead means you're safe
and nobody
will bully you or need you any more.

Maybe I Should Give It a Try

Maybe I should give it a try,
maybe I should take a chance and go for it,
weep, wail,
see what happens next,
cry for him,
for her,
and cry for everyone,
cry for all the little chopped-up mealie-worms
dying in their thousands in the mealie,
cry for carports,

cry for billionaires,
cry for lynx in diamond-studded harnesses,
cry for polyps,
cry for stuffed hawks,
cry for Sunbeam Talbots,
cry for Thunder Thighs,
cry for half-dazed wasps,
for divorcees,
cry for Tito, cry for Sophia Loren
throwing Hungarian sausages into the sea,
cry for Roger Federer,
cry for me,
horizontal in the icy water,
skinny-dipping for the broken-hearted,
cry, weep, wail,
eat the chocolate
approaching from the East
in rattling lorries.

My Mother Playing Tennis

Dressed in long white skirts,
she seemed to float,
and being dead's the same,
it's so *relaxed*,
at least
that's what the living seem to think.

Babs

She stinks of cigarettes,
she's obese,
she spends her days eating and smoking
and stubs her cigarettes out in her custard
and anyway she doesn't even eat,
she spends her days sucking pills instead
and burning little holes in her nightdress,
she lives on nothing but the pills and cake,
her bed is like a car park full of crumbs
in which she turns away and falls apart,
I sit beside her getting on her nerves,
I ask her if she's frightened,
she says yes,
she doesn't want my pity,
she wants morphine,
morphine like a woman in a suit
kissing her until she can't breathe,
she doesn't need to breathe,
she's bit the dust,
there's only me,
fidgeting about,
there's only me
waiting for the angels
and wondering how angels groom their wings.

The Dead

I know two things about the dead,
they're dead
and of no use to anyone but strangers
who say a prayer
and turn them inside out.

Telepathy

Where's he living,
is he still alive,
would I even like him if he is,
why do I keep thinking of him suddenly,
telepathy,
how does that work,
let's be honest
he was never handsome
but he was mine
and nothing if not kind,
why don't I just send him a card,
find out where he lives
and send a card,
nothing heavy,
just a simple card,
a cat, a jug, something like that,
and no, I'd never say this in the card,
but maybe it's his absence I'm in love with,
in which his presence is beatified,
aloof, serene, adored
and platinum blond.

The Room

She couldn't have been less like her daughter,
like me, in other words,
who questions everything
like why do I keep thinking of the room
and why am I so frightened of him touching me
that hours go by that might as well be centuries
and why can't I be graceful like my mother,
why can't I be calm and incorruptible,
why can't I be cool,
like quartz or ice,
cool, alluring, fierce,
like orange snow,
like sand from the Sahara
in Siberia,
it's not as if I'm sick
or don't know how,
it's not as if I haven't seen her dying
and haven't seen her smiling
like a guest
who thanks her hostess
as she leaves the room,
it's not as if I'm not a grown woman
whose mother I can never hurt again.

Her Being Dead

Her being dead,
how can I put this,
my mother being dead
makes perfect sense,
her having lived's
God's gift to the sky.

MY SPANISH SWIMSUIT

The Earwig

The earwig from the cupboard
makes a dash for it
and ends up out of breath
inside my pillow,
praying to be turned into fur.

My Little Sister

Please be gentle with your little dog.
She'll grow up like my little sister otherwise,
who always looks haunted
for some reason.

The Box of Assorted Plasters

I'd no idea how tiny they would be.
I didn't know they *could* be so tiny.

Tea on the Lawn

Tea on the lawn? Madeira cake?
Forget it.
Commiserating?
As I say, *forget it*.

My Father, God

I know he isn't God
but he's *like* God.
I imagine God
to be more tolerant.

Betrayed

The word that makes most sense
is *betrayed*.
He is my father
and I am *betrayed*.

Saluki

I live with fear
like another child
might live with their Saluki, for example.

Shadow

I see his shadow
cross my bedroom wall.
I say I'm sorry
but I'm not sorry.

Which Is Worse?

Which is worse – to age
or to try *not* to age?
My father, for example.
The dyed hair.

My Pet

I have a pet.
My pet is called Fear.
She lies beside me in my bed at night.

Smarties

A little girl appears
and drops her Smarties
which my father crushes
with his wheelchair
but the girl refuses to cry.

Adults

The adults like to sit on rocks
and wait

but as soon as I reach the rocks
they wander off.

My Mother and Small Children

My mother does *not like* the way small children
are *constantly being picked up.*

Courting

Courting is called *courting*
and her boyfriends,
some of whom I spy on,
are called *suitors*.

Ringlets

Ringlets, they are called.
I've always hated them.
My father, on the other hand,
adores them.

My Father

He doesn't deserve to be mine
and to be my father,
and he doesn't deserve to be loved,
and he isn't loved.

Rabbits

I don't dislike everyone,
far from it,
as long as they have never hurt a rabbit.

The Head of the Table

Even God himself
might go and sit
somewhere else
but my father? Never!

The Girls in the Churchyard

My father is a terrifying man.
He terrifies us both.
As does hers.
And that's why we are playing in the churchyard.

My Spanish Swimsuit

As soon as he admires my Spanish swimsuit
I know I'll never wear it again.

Shoulders

Everyone assumes he is my father
but Shoulders is actually my brother.

Yes to the Carpenter

No to men with chocolates in their pockets,
to men who wink –
but yes to the carpenter
who keeps his pencil tucked behind his ear.

My Father's Rabbit

Not everybody wants to be loved,
not everybody wants to be the rabbit
he catches in his trap by the paw.

I'm Sorry It Has Had to Be Like This

I'm sorry it has had to be like this,
is what they say,
or what they long to say,
but they can't,
I'm sorry but they can't.

Moths

The moths that make their home
inside our curtains
are spared from knowing
what the man has done.

My Girlfriends' Boyfriends

Just as all my boyfriends are my girlfriends',
the letters of *ungodliest* spell *longitudes*.

My Father Is Right

You'll never guess where *I've* been!
says my father
and he is right,
I never do guess.

The Lonely Dog in the Empty House

When they took the body away
the dog refused to move
and the mourners
left her there and never came back.

THE CHAUFFEUR

Attention is the prayer of the soul.

ARAB PROVERB

Tiny Girls Singing Hymns

The tiny girls singing hymns ask *Why*,
why does no one come to our rescue,
why does no one dare to acknowledge
that it is fear that forces us to sing?
My sister is so stupefied by fear
she doesn't understand a word she's singing.

Girls in Shorts

My sister wears long skirts or long dresses.
I however like to wear shorts.
She doesn't really like girls in shorts.
Men in shorts? Yes – if they play tennis!
Only joking. She can't stand tennis.
Women who wear shorts? I don't think so!
(unless they wear them under their pyjamas
in order to soak up any drips).

The Draughtsman

He draws her and he draws her and he draws her
whether she likes it or not.
And she does. Until it is too late.
I refuse. He won't betray *me*!

Fish

We say it's love but we know it's fear,
we know it's fear that drives my sister on,
on into the arms she hopes will hold her;
that chill her body like the arms of fish.

Shells

Everyone is so argumentative!
We never listen to a word she says.
We crush her like a person made of shells.
We file past her on our way to work –
chins up, stomachs in – and nobody
takes the time to even say goodbye.
She listens as we crunch across the gravel,
she listens as the wheels of the cars
crunch along the drive to the motorway.
She's nothing but a heap of broken shells
that cut you if you touch them, so we don't.

The Land of Fun

When I'm in the same room as her,
or when she's in the same room as me,
I become arrogant and mean,
I don't know why I do but I do.
Such forlornness! I'm like *Buzz off* –
contaminate my land of fun no further!

My Sister's Bedroom

Half of it – because her mother tells her
not to stand *anywhere near the window*
where somebody could see her from the street –
my sister never dares to venture into.

Ducks

Nobody *wants* to have bad teeth,
least of all my sister, who's not perfect
(no one is) but who aspires to be,
(the aspiration's ruining her life!).
I don't mean really bad, I just mean one,
one rogue tooth that's slightly in the way,
a bit too big, like toenails sometimes are
(that wives are there to tell men how to cut!)
but anyway a tooth is not a toenail,
she can't just clip it level like a hedge,
a tooth is not a hedge that can be ducks –
peacocks, ducks, anything you fancy!

Rotty the Rottweiler

Imagine being locked up with a Rottweiler
when anyway you're terrified of Rottweilers;
people smile and call her 'Rotty' but
you do not trust that Rottweiler one bit!
That slobberer of slobber in hot laps,
cruncher of red bodies of small mammals,
hoarder of dead dolls and cattle bones!
What I'm trying to say is Just imagine
my sister being locked up with *me*!

Smile, Smile

Don't even think about that *smile, smile!*
The kind of adult that she hopes to be
is much too wise, too serious to smile.
Unless we mean that other kind of smile
that smiles at the world *as it is*
and not as people *feel it to be*;
it's like she hopes to be a sort of seer,
somebody who sees the unseen.

Marquetry

I'm not remotely interested in marquetry!
I mean, what even *is* marquetry?
She does these courses, *How to Change Your Life*,
stuff like that; I, however, luckily,
am one of those (apparently now rare)
women who don't mind being women.

I Send My Sister Cards

I send my sister cards when it suits me;
it doesn't suit me very often; latterly
it hasn't really suited me at all,
I'm busy, I've run out of cards, and anyway
sending cards will only stir things up –
and anyway enough about myself!
Hind legs. Donkey. Sorry. Bended knee.

Smile, Smile, Smile

Smile! smile! smile! But she can't.
I mean how sad is that? Or is it me?
Am I just imagining she can't?
Because she can't smile around me?
I'm trying but her face will *not* smile.
Let's start again: she is neat and slim
(all that 'puppy fat' has long gone)
with straight black hair (so, yes, it's *not* like mine!),
her hazel eyes have got a haunted look;
her hands are small and white like the hands
a little queen might wave (but her skin,
I'm sorry but her skin is quite sallow,
her mother seems to think her skin's *disgraceful*,
her future husband certainly does,
he pays for it to be 'professionally cleaned'!
I can see it now: white room.
Teams of men in goggles pick at pores.
It's not as if she's dirty. She is not:

she is cleaned not just once but every day,
cleaned and whitened, by an Unseen Hand.)
He doesn't like the muddy cows either
that peer at him through the muddy hedge.
(I prefer the cows to the wedding guests
that mill about like insolent raptors.)

The Wedding-dress

The wedding-dress is going *Don't ask me!*
I don't know what she's doing either!

In the Hotel Bedroom Something Soft

In the hotel bedroom something soft
glides towards her from the dead bouquets,
it rambles through her hair and round her ears,
it wraps its massive foot around the breast
in which her heart, once so pure, is trembling.

Hippo

Have you ever noticed what kind eyes
a hippo has? Her eyes are like that.
That's not to say her *face* is like a hippo's
because it's not. Just the kind eyes.
The kind yet rather miserable eyes.

Ann

Does my sister have any friends?
Of course she does! Wonderful friends!
They send each other cards and share their sorrows,
they feed the birds (but draw the line at Ann
who walks across my bed every evening
on her way to catch herself some flies).

The Suitcase

She stands there like an orphan with a suitcase
but without the suitcase. So forlorn!
She stands and waits – for what, she does not know –
she stands until she has to sit down,
she's sinking down into someone's sitting-room,
what she needs is this, a little suitcase,
a little suitcase she can call her own
filled with coloured pencils and a pencil sharpener
so she can sit and draw coloured ponies
eating coloured flowers in coloured meadows
where coloured butterflies with Latin names
are spreading their improbably large wings
across the petals, to her heart's content;
what she needs is friendly men and women
telling her in no uncertain terms
that she is not a doormat, she's a woman,
a lovable – yes, lovable – woman.

Tommy

When he's 'done his business' in the tray
(just don't do it in the pot plants, Tommy!)
he grabs another tasty potted shrimp
before retiring to the laundry basket.

Those Who Choose Not to Have Husbands

Those who choose not to have husbands,
fair enough, O.K., but for G.,
not having one makes her feel repulsive.

Our Sparkling Eyes

Timidity puts people off:
when everybody else is *being sociable*
the timid person gets in the way.
She makes us feel judged. Our sparkling eyes
look at her as if we don't need her.

Queue

When he sees me first in queue
yet again, he says *Your poor sister!*

My Sister's Nipples

Is it true one of them is hairy?
And even if it is, what's wrong with that?
She says *These little biscuits are delicious!*
No they're not. They taste of dried pain.

Tinkle, Tinkle

Humility is all very well
but somebody is taking it too far:
she's like a distant valley lost in mist,
a dream of tinkling goats without the goats.

Tea-time

She brings us tea – with tea from the teapot
and chocolate biscuits from the biscuit tin –
and after tea she goes upstairs to scream.

She Moves Away

She moves away and never comes back
and never says goodbye to her mother,
whether at the house or at the hospital.
What did someone do? We don't know.

Horses' Ears

Anything that's pleasurable – let's say
fondling horses' ears – is now less so.

St Petersburg

I can force my sister to do anything!
Smile, smile, smile! But she won't.
On the contrary, she seems afraid.
Even, look, the collar of her nightie,
even the minuscule pink slippers
she likes to think of as her ballet pumps,
even her teabags, look afraid.
St Petersburg? Vienna? *No way!*

The Photograph

In the end they had to dismantle it –
the fairy lights, the shells, the dead flowers –
but what to do with the photograph?
Bin it is the answer. Quietly bin it.

Wild Horses

How to thank them, how to thank the mourners
for giving her, my sister, their attention;
how to not be me, the sort of person
who couldn't even sit and hold her hand,
wasn't that the least I could do,
how come I couldn't even do that,
all the others did, but not me?
Wild horses. Pain. Let's just say
my sister's better off with her Maker
and both are better off without me.

Georges

It was only after she had died,
and after Georges had died, that I was told
that Georges had been his lover; that her father
had named his daughter after his lover.

Lips

When they were alive it was confusing.
Now they're dead it is not confusing.
Or no more so than lips of different colours
and different thicknesses are confusing.

Gladioli

And all the time she seemed to be saying
Stop being happy! So I stopped.
And everything went pear-shaped. And now
I'm like a gladiolus or a mouse
enjoying being singular again.

GIRLS WITHOUT HAMSTERS

1 | Dancing Lessons for the Very Shy

The Visitor (1)

My visitor is a handsome spider,
six-foot tall and elegantly dressed,
who perches on the arm of my sofa
saying nothing, as a spider must.

Dawn

Half-asleep,
at dawn,
I see a spider
whose tiny face
is trying not to cry.

The Little Beanie

So this is what it's like
to see a spider
in a little beanie
on my doorstep.

The Handsome Spider

I called the spider handsome
but he's not.
Which is fine.
I don't like handsome spiders.

So Tiny and Forlorn

Because it looks so tiny and forlorn,
his face is like the face of a spider –
a spider who, having been to smiling classes,
is trying out his very first smile.

The Visitor (2)

My visitor – how odd – is here again,
elegantly dressed,
and saying nothing,
the way a monk or nun might say nothing.

The Sofa

Imagine a spider made of glass,
a six-foot spider made of spun glass;
imagine you're a person who loves spiders
and imagine sitting very close beside it.

The Wasp

I'm sorry but I couldn't resist
but now I'm thinking, like I knew I would,
that I was wrong,
that I have gone too far,
I think about you far too much,
I'm sorry,
it isn't fair on you or on me,
I want to help you but I don't know how,
you're six-foot tall and trying not to cry,
they say it's good to cry,
I never cry,
I never cried when my father died,
I hoped and prayed he'd never come back,
I only cry when I'm overjoyed,
I'm overjoyed today to see you now,
but being 'overjoyed''s not always helpful,
at least that's what I'm guessing they would say,
and what I really want to do is squeeze you,
squeeze you till your tears roll down like honey
rolling down the back of a spoon,
the way it makes its way very slowly,

when no one's watching,
no one but a wasp
watching from a nearby sugar-sprinkler.

The Top Two Things I Like about You

The top two things
I like about you are:
your attitude to sex
and your hamster.

The Bath (1)

Half-asleep in the empty house,
I close my eyes
and listen to the bubbles
breathing their contented little breaths.

I Know It Isn't Right

I know it isn't right
for me to hug you
but if it was
I would hug you now.

Cats in Crates

It feels wrong and when it feels wrong
I see not you and me but cats in crates,
strafed by light,
as far as the eye can see.

The Most Important Thing

The most important thing is the touch,
the touch with which I want to touch your hand,

but only when I'm certain that you want me to,
which I'm certain I will never be.

A Person with a Key

I check the locks of crates of bony cats.
Although I know it's wrong, I check the locks.

The Visitor (3)

It's already dark when the visitor
turns up on my doorstep with a suitcase,

or anyhow it feels like a suitcase
that, as he talks, I can peep inside.

The Crane

I have been entrusted with a crane
on condition nobody must know
and nobody must touch it or offend it
and every night at supper I must sing to it
because that's just the kind of bird it is.

The Ginger Cat

It watches us for a long time
and then it walks away
without a word,
leaving us alone with its absence.

Us

Just you and me today?
I don't think so.
There is also *us*
which makes us shy.

The Fly

Like a fly
walking on a fish,
I almost touched your hand,
then changed my mind.

The Suitcase

You open your imaginary suitcase
to show me your imaginary collection
of hundreds of imaginary pins'
imaginary and glittering entanglements.

Elephants

When elephants are warm
they smell of cake;
when you are warm,
you smell of cake too.

The Man with a Pomegranate

Please don't use your knife.
Use your fingers,
your beautiful and prehensile fingers.

The Coat

How can I possibly be missing him
when I never see him in the first place?
I'm like a girl who bursts into tears
on finding there's no fledgling in her pocket!

The Giraffe

If I saw the ghost of a giraffe
gliding down the avenue towards me

if I saw him slowing down, and stopping,
if I saw him leaning down to talk to me,

I wouldn't know what to say or do
and neither did I know when I saw you.

The Hat

Maybe I liked him because of the tiny hat –
or maybe I liked him *in spite of* the tiny hat;
and maybe it doesn't matter, it's only a hat!

(But at that time, of course, I'd no idea
why you wore that tiny hat that night,
pulled right down so I could hardly see you.)

Tenderness

Like a shoal of fish in the sea
the words I need suddenly change direction

and head off somewhere else as if to say
Tenderness? Don't even *think* about it!

The Visitor (4)

To me, you're not quite you,
you are the visitor,

a stranger from another land who visits,
now and then,

for no apparent reason,
bringing small and medium-sized presents.

When I Saw You in the Street I Fled

I fled because I wanted to see you.
I wanted to see you *very much*.
To lift you up as if you were a doll
and swing you round
but I mustn't do that.

Silence

My driver is driving the car
down the road to the motorway.

He drives in silence.
You are out of sight.

The Man I Mustn't Meet

I mustn't meet the man I mustn't meet,
I mustn't meet him for his own good,

he needs to be the kind of man he is
and not the kind he thinks he ought to be,

he needs to get, in other words, to get
as far away from me as he can get.

The Path to the Woods

Every day the drivers drive their lorries
and every day I walk to the woods

in order not to have to meet the man
I keep away from for his own good.

Knees

You're like a spider made of eyes and knees.
Please don't be afraid to sit still.

Although You're Shy

Although you're shy,
although you hardly know me,
see if you can manage a whisper
if I *promise* I will block my ears.

The Dachshund

She used to have a dog,
but it bit her
and now, she says,
she doesn't see the point.
She doesn't even see the point of men!
After tea, I suggest a snail.

The Snail

I used to keep a snail in a tank,
a long glass fishtank, all along one wall.
I tried to give him everything he needed
and make his life as comfortable as possible.
The first thing I would do every morning
was see where he had got to in the night,
I'd peer into his little faceless face
and wonder where he came from and how old he was
and whether he could dream, or feel lonely,
and all the time I knew him and cared for him

he never complained; on the contrary,
he seemed quite happy in his glass home
and didn't seem to mind being watched,
or being offered curious fruits;
courteous and grateful, he would sit
beside his little rock for hours on end
as if to say, or chant, *who needs plans?*
It's true he wasn't cheerful exactly
but to me he was, and always will be,
sinless and beautiful, like you.

What I Did When I Saw You Again After So Long

I suddenly lurched sideways
like the bus
carrying a choir to a wedding
that toppled over into a ravine.

Swimming at Dawn

As I swim along in my underwear
I'm feeling over-dressed
and unlike fish.

Attention

He gives us His attention
all the time
but do we want it,
necessarily?

The Bath (2)

But now the bath is cold
and getting colder;
the water's weighing down my breasts
like weed.

Her Only Son

They tell me that his mother
had one son
she dedicated her short life
to loving.

Violins

I'm sitting on the sofa
in the dark
beside a man
with legs like a spider's
that feel like the sound of violins.

Your Rock

She longs to be much younger and more beautiful.
She longs to be more tender and restrained.
She longs to be your *rock* – if a rock
can also be tender and restrained.
Most of all, she longs to be beside you.
(When I say 'she' I mean me.)

Peacefully Tucked Away

Please can someone scoop it all up
and peacefully tuck it away in another dimension.
Answer (in a sort of booming voice):
No, they can't! Tuck it away yourself!

My Life with You

My life with you's like life inside an airing-cupboard –
and airing-cupboards don't have any air!
And neither are they likely to be offering
dancing lessons for the very shy.

One Hundred Words

By the time we part
we will have learnt
one hundred words
for when it's all over.

Never Love a Mathematician

Never love a mathematician
and never be alone with a crane,
never hope it won't when it will –
and never breathe a word to a soul.

Grasses

How come there is a family of grasses
standing by my bed as if they know me,

as if they've come to tell me they're so thin
because they've stopped pretending to be trees?

just as you, alone at home, have stopped
pretending to be anyone but you:

if you need to walk, you need to walk;
if you need to grieve, you need to grieve;

if you need to move without moving,
alone and incorruptible, you sleep.

Precious Jewels

Everybody dies.
They can't help it.
Even mothers die.
Especially mothers.
Mothers die like flies –
the kind of flies
that shine like jewels
in the depths of mines.

Most of the Time

Most of the time
I'm not aware of my clothes
brushing against my skin
but sometimes I am.

Socks in the Snow

Outside in the dark
two pairs of socks
are hanging by their toes
in the snow.

If You Were a Pig

If you were a pig or a warthog
I could fling my arms
round your neck;

and if I was a warthog as well
we wouldn't be so shy –
but I'm not.

Everything Makes Me Think of You

Even my own nose in the snow
makes me think of you
because you're thin –

and what you need, I realise now, is *warmth*,
my mission is to make you feel *warm*,
warm and safe, I understand that now –

you keep to nooks and crannies
like a spider
forever rearranging its long legs.

The Enchantment

I don't know how or why you have enchanted me,
or why I need to know,
but I do;
after all, we couldn't be more different,
you yourself are so restrained and tender –
and, I'm ashamed to say,
I feel afraid.

Dancing Lessons for the Advanced in Age
by Bohumil Hrabal

I can take the dogs to the library
but not if I am going to the shops.
Either way, it's not what you think.

The Visitor (5)

How can I keep thinking I am missing you
when anyway I hardly ever see you?
The answer is I don't want to see you:
I only want to think maybe I might.

In a Calm Way

I'm trying to speak of you in a calm,
to speak of you in a calm way –
to speak of you as 'him', it's more respectful –
and I am trying to be more respectful.

The Person on Our Right

The person on our right's eating fish –
and when somebody's eating fish
I can't think straight.

The Rat

My brain is like a rat in a wheel
and even when I'm floating upside down
its tiny paws
keep going till they're raw.

Articulated Lorries

Some people need articulated lorries,
some people need dazzling white beaches,
some people need poodles; as for me,
I need to be alone and in the dark.

The Bath (3)

Nothing but the sound of the bubbles
dying their hopeless little deaths.

The Clock

To the clock,
it's going anti-clockwise
and so, to me,
I'm going anti-clockwise.

Nose

The nose I call a snout when I'm a pig,
when I'm a woman, senses early snow.

Shrieks of Laughter from Inside the House

And afterwards we heard, or thought we heard,
shrieks of laughter from inside the house
we couldn't reach because of all the snow
piled up in drifts on every side.

Completely Out of the Blue

So, yes, I fell in love with this person,
and such an inappropriate kind of person,
and such an inappropriate kind of love,
a kind of love we couldn't understand,
completely out of the blue,
it was incredible –

a kind of love that we can laugh at now,
now that it's more…what? more understandable?
like the love of hamsters, for example,
a pair of hamsters chatting in the sun;
we laugh – but, like all love,
it's still incredible.

2 | My Mother's Knives

T.

Nobody must know
it is him,

it is T.,
with whom I am obsessed.

Mole

I live in darkness
like the humble mole,

the sweet, bewitching darkness
of not knowing him.

My Mother's Knives

As my mother's daughter, I was taught
always to respect my mother's knives.

Also to respect my mother's secrets.
And to get some secrets of my own.

The Older Woman

The older woman who becomes obsessed
by a younger man is an idiot –

she may think she is cool
but she's an idiot.

T.'s Room

Sometimes I picture his room
(I know I shouldn't but I sometimes do),

sometimes I picture a figure
disappearing down a winding stair

and sometimes I picture his skin
(but without picturing me touching it).

Bucket

Like a little chick
that cheeps at anything –

it could be something odd
like a bucket –

and follows it around,
I follow T.

(T. is not and never will be
a bucket,

he couldn't be *less*
like a bucket,

what I'm trying to say is
it's just weird.)

Please Forgive Me

I run towards him –
at the same time

saying to myself
Please forgive me.

Tiers of Expensive Trainers

What I need is what the others have –
tiers of expensive trainers, perfect teeth –

not certain things I don't want to think about.
I don't know why I don't but I don't.

I Worry

I worry, when he's quiet,
I've upset him –

but no, I needn't worry,
he's just shy.

The Visitor

Some of its ungainly legs
were missing

and now a bird
has probably got it.

Into the Depths of the Sea

Although he's so fastidious
and elegant,

which makes him seem aloof,
his eyes are kind:

I gaze into his eyes
like a suicide

might gaze
into the depths of the sea.

His Tiny Mouth

His tiny mouth
can no more speak than sing,

or that's what I believed
but I was wrong.

Through the Damp Woods

Elongated, weightless
and obsessed,

the spider prances
through the damp woods.

Bedtime

When he comes and sits beside my bed,
his skinny legs so thin
they wave like hairs,

I want to say
I am afraid of hurting him
but I don't know how to begin.

People Won't Like It

If you're what they call
'an older woman'

who rabbits on
about 'relationships',

you're going to find
people won't like it.

Chick

All I do
is scurry after him –

cheep, cheep, cheep –
until I fall over.

Fish

Older women's secrets are like fish
cruising in the depths of a lake;

ugly fish with eyes that can't see;
that live in darkness without knowing why.

Paint

This person is a person,
he's not paint

waiting in some shed
for me to paint with.

What Is Longing?

Longing's being battered
till I'm raw –

but what I'm longing *for*
I've no idea.

Beetles

I could be a spider too and pounce
on passing beetles with the hairy legs

that complement
my slinky little dresses.

Heron

Because he is a cautious
sort of person
he hides himself away

like the heron
dreaming in the rushes
by the lake.

Certain Older Women

Older women,
like besotted chicks,

follow men around
as if they're buckets –

certain older women,
I should say,

follow *certain* men
(in my case, T.).

Hope

If I ever sense
a tiny hope

stirring in the depths,
I must whack it.

A Precious Living Man

Spider, bucket,
anything will do –

but not, please not,
a precious living man.

And to Agree

They need to be well-mannered and serene
and – most important –
scrupulously clean;

they must not talk,
their job is to listen
when other people talk, and to agree.

My Father

He never moved
or talked to me

but T.
never stops moving,

like a spider
who darts across the faces of the blessed.

Actually,
let's not mention fathers.

Confessions of a Fly

I tiptoe round the room
like a fly

that wishes she was lovely
and less murderous.

The Courting Spider Purrs

Alert and patient
in the chilly woods,

he rubs his palps together
and he purrs.

Cranny

Every night,
on sixteen ghostly legs,
we'll dance until we're dizzy
and at dawn

we'll find a little cranny
to collapse in,
helpless not with longing
but with laughter.

Dreams

Let's celebrate
their hopeless little deaths –

the hopeless little deaths
of the dreams

but also, in due course,
of the women

who dream the little dreams,
who can find

nobody to whom
they can offer them.

Mouse

I hesitate to greet him –
like a mouse

alone at night
without a star to guide her.

Round and Round the Woods

Round and round the woods
like a murderer

(or someone who has witnessed
a murder,

someone who is terrified
of love,

who needs to move
as quietly as she can)

round and round the woods
I follow T.;

I follow T.
as quietly as I can

and hope and pray
he never looks back.

If T. Is Like a God

If T. is like a god, he's like a god
who doesn't even know he's a god,

and he must never know, and I must act
normal, if not cold, at all times.

When Older Women Talk About Their Lovers

When older women talk about their lovers
I try and change the subject
to their dogs

or, better still, their dresses –
their limp rows
of almost identical dresses.

Legs

If I spotted T.
in the undergrowth

my skinny legs
would twitch like a nose

and some of them
would probably fall off.

Every Time You Move

If you're what they call
'an older woman',

every time you move
you're in their way.

Cranefly

But I can no more ask
the leggy cranefly

how he's getting on
in my shower-room

than ask the man
to come inside and tell me

what it is
that makes him look so sad.

T. on the Beach

It's him, it's him,
happy and untouchable,
standing on the palms of his hands.

I thought he couldn't speak
but I was wrong.
He's speaking with the language of his steadiness.

When He's Quiet

When he's quiet
I worry I've upset him

but no, I must remember:
he's just shy.

Dog

He turns up on my doorstep
like a dog.

He creeps inside…
Tell me where it hurts.

My Obsession with T.

It wasn't really T.
I was obsessed by

but someone else entirely
I invented

while T. himself,
T. is still here,

but even sweeter,
if you can imagine.

The Acrobat

Although he's upside down,
and it's snowing,

he's so relaxed
he looks as if he's floating

somewhere where there's no such thing
as loss.

3 | The Passion Fruit Hotel

Record-breaking Kisses

We called the cabin PASSION FRUIT HOTEL
and it was here me and my best friend

experienced our record-breaking kisses.
Hers was on the lips, or so she said;

mine was on the neck, and was my first.
We didn't know the name of the boy

(and it was always him) but we suspected
that, if we did, everything would change –

that we would have to speak, for example,
and no one spoke in PASSION FRUIT HOTEL.

My Mother and Hotels

Hotels, to her, were never to be trusted.
And nor was passion – certainly not!

(except, perhaps, men's passion for topiary,
the neighbour's, for example, for his peacock.)

The Passion Flower Hotel

The day I read *The Passion Flower Hotel* –
and I didn't even read it! – was the day

something died, something like a bird
I hadn't even realised had been singing.

The House on the Hill

Imagine that you're on a long journey,
sitting in a train, in a window seat,
when suddenly you see, in the distance,

a curious little house you seem to recognise,
a house you think you slept in as a child,
standing by itself on a hill...

and then the train continues on its way,
leaving you confused about what happened:
that was how I felt when I met T.

And Be Ye Lift Up, Ye Everlasting Doors

And later, when I saw him walking past
(completely out of the blue! I couldn't believe it!)

I felt my spirits being lifted up
as surely as those everlasting doors.

My Mother Was Right

Passion? At your age? said my niece
glaring at me like I was nuts.

(Obviously my mother was right:
passion is never to be mentioned.)

The Lovesick Toad

The spider, though polite, walks straight past
and disappears into a nearby hedge.

The toad, however, sits and waits for him,
possibly misled by his politeness.

Crayfish

He's like the crunchy pastries shaped like crayfish
(unexpected, sweet and unpronounceable);
he's like a river made of arms and legs;

he's like the ships that pass in the night,
king-sized towels, cabins on the beach –
so yes, I am besotted, I can't help it!

And if I try and think of something else
up he pops like trout or like a goblin
I long to tickle but I don't know how.

Ducklings

In the dream, I offered him fried ducklings
and slowly, without looking up, he spoke;

he spoke, but, as he spoke, he was crying
and I couldn't understand a word he said.

The Goose

They fed him through a tube like a goose
until he reached a pre-determined weight
and then they sent him home –

to be returned,
several weeks later, by his parents,
one on either side, to stop his falling.

Way Up in the Heavens

Can't they understand he's way above them,
he's like a bird they only dream they know,

he's like a bird way up in the heavens
or, at the very least, on a tree?

Fathers and Sons

No one's saying fathers and sons
should keep in touch. No one's saying that.

Honky

I've got a wooden goose that can honk;
a goose my uncle made I've still got.

The only thing that Honky can't do,
that T. can do, and will do, is die.

Chandeliers

I hang them in what used to be the stables
where pulsing sprinklers
play on them all day

and keep them softly shimmering
like thoroughbreds –
and keep my little mouth shut about T.

Margaret

Margaret was his first, his only love.
He'd kiss her on the snout

and she would tremble
and, gratefully, as she trembled, grunt.

Sunday Afternoon at the Beach

While getting changed,
I see that T. is crying

but whereas he is clothed
I am naked.

T.'s Neck

If he were a dog and not a man
I'd bury my fat face in his neck.

What People Think About

Older women think about each other.
Younger women think about themselves.
Men, however, think about things.
I, myself, think about T.

The Slug

It drags its single foot
across my skin

like something homeless
looking for a home;

it digs its little chin
into my neck

as if to say
infatuate, infatuate.

Shoebill

I'm writing this in a small hotel
while balancing a shoebill on my head

and, if I try and shake him off, he shrieks –
and, OK, if I'm honest, I would miss him.

I'm like this tick, embedded in his foot:
I feed off his intoxicating juices.

My Friend T.

T. is not exactly a friend –
but in a way you could say he is,

the way that time is friend to the clock,
music to the fingers of the blind.

Wiry

I want to call him wiry but wiry
doesn't sound adorable enough.

And not just me –
everyone adores him,

the way intransigent fleas
adore fur.

The Holiday

Because I was so desperate to distract myself
I came out here – *miles away!*

And have I got distracted? I have not.
Maybe T. has come up here too!

The Lizard

Lounging by the pool,
I saw a lizard

and knew at once
I'd never been so fat.

The Oyster

The way I'm feeling now about T.,
it feels too despondent to be passion,

it feels like an oyster on a plate
that's dreaming of its home in the ocean.

Soft Upturned Bellies

Did you know that crows collect frogs,
flip them over,
stab their upturned bellies
and peck their innards out?

just as T.
(my *dream* of T., that is,
if dreams have beaks)
disembowels me.

My Mother's Voice

My mother always begged me to stop
and now she's gone I beg myself myself.

And does it help? No.
It makes it worse.

The Woman in Tiny Shorts

The fact that she was wearing tiny shorts
made me want to murder her unfortunately.

My Boring Uncle

I used to think my uncle was boring
but now I see the point of being boring,

of drifting, in expensive leather slippers,
in and out of rooms until you drop.

What I Really Want to Know

What I really want to know is this:
what does T. think about *me*?

And am I right in thinking he is thinking
I'm just some prissy *pain in the neck*?

And do I really want to know?
I don't.

For Amy whose advice I am ashamed to say I rarely follow.
Also for Pearl: KOI 29, Pearl?

Q: What's your speck on the horizon, Jos, that distant goal that inspires you and your team?

JOS DE BLOCK: Not all that inspired by specks.

The Red MG

A red MG draws up outside her door.
Just a little trip to the vintner.
She knows what people think.
Well, they can think it.
Vera can look after herself!
Can and does. She's making it quite clear
all she needs is to locate the door
for which her being special is the key.
She dabs some powder on her slender nose
and steps across the hall like Belafonte –
like Belafonte meets the Milky Way.

The Fox

Let's start from the beginning. (He's a man
who's expert in beginnings and beginners!
Not that they're beginners. We know that.
Let's just say it's like they wish they were.)
He's wily, suave and penniless. A fox.
A handsome silver fox, obviously –
who's ordered some camellias for her birthday.
(He's not quite sure what camellias are
but anyhow he's hoping she'll think *opera*!)

The Blanket

In the cosy bathroom of the bungalow
she pulls her nightie off and her vest
and chucks them in the corner like the wind.
Her neighbour says he 'feels the cold'. *Good!*
(If only she would wrap him in that blanket
she wraps around her waist on the balcony;
if only she would give a little wave,
just a *flick*, how hard can that be?)

Quivering Jelly

Vera's one of those annoying people
('annoying', did I say? Not even close!)
who never listens to a word you say.
Also, she expects you to be smart.
(Just be sure you're not as smart as Vera!)
So, yes, she can be harsh, like a mountain-top;
yes, she can reduce you to a jelly.
Your only hope is *never to wear jeans*
and regularly send her camellias.

A New Pair of Shorts

A balding figure steps from the pavilion
wearing shorts, in spite of the rain.
It's time to go back in where his wife
is cramming her enormous face with fudge,
enormous like a fluffy white bath towel.
Let's not forget how tired a wife can be –
saintly, freshly-manicured but *tired*.
(She's hoping he will sleep like a log.)
Not so Vera. Vera understands him.
At last, she thinks, *here we have a man*
who knows what he is doing! But he doesn't.
He's holding to his chest a brown parcel
containing shorts he's never going to wear.

Lime-ade

She's not a doll! She grabs the nasty scissors,
tugs the woman's hand (some blood is drawn),
grabs her bag and briskly leaves the room,
sorry, leaves the *salon*, and the hairdresser,
sorry, and the *stylist*'s leaving too,
she wants to reprimand her, but the client,
beady-eyed and hot, is having none of it,
she wants to be alone with her juice,
her toxic-looking, beryl-green juice
whose phosphorescence calls her by her name
and tells her to get back to her bungalow,
to never let herself be touched again,
brushed against, by disinfected pinafores
she wouldn't be seen *dead* even sniffing,
let alone sitting in a salon with.
She doesn't need pampering, forget it!
She's not a poodle, she's a grown woman!
She leaves at once for her bungalow,
her china and her antique clocks, her literature,
literature that *broadens the mind*,
the broadened mind that throbs inside the body
that's striding through the streets and up the steps
to rooms like empty graves
or still waters.

Men in Shorts

Vera thinks she does but she doesn't.
She strides along (Vera is *determined*
to stride along like she always has done),
she strides along on her sturdy legs
and chats away to everyone she meets
as if it's all OK but it's not.
Vera is unable to tolerate
being who she fears she thinks she might be.
A group of men in shorts comes along.
She smiles at them brightly. Her sad eyes
let her smiles down every time.

Duckling

Now she's 'getting on', as they say,
it's time to start pleasing herself.
Obviously she doesn't like children
or dogs or cats or anything like that
but more than once she has surprised her doctor
by twiddling a lock of his hair.
Another time she walked across the park
and purposefully trampled on a duckling.
And now she turns the greasy grill *full on*.
(Vera likes eating but not waiting!)

Oral Sex

When she's put the tablecloth away
she slips into her room for a rest
and dreams she's being blown to bits by gunners
who in their private lives are quite shy.
She tells them callisthenics keeps her flexible –
and prays there's no such thing as oral sex.

The China Doll

The neighbour and his wife have got no children
or anyway there's no sign of children,
unless the china doll is a sign
that glares at her from an upstairs window
as if to say *to smile is obscene*;
it's like the sort of person, like her husband,
who wouldn't even smile for the Queen.

Walkies

Her husband should have been a Chihuahua
then Vera could have stroked him and brushed him
and taken him for walks in the park
and dressed him in a bow, but he wasn't.
And anyway she doesn't like dogs...
She's lying in her bath getting cold.
Outside, in the sunshine, she can hear
sixteen paws crunch across the gravel.
Her neighbour will be hiding in his shed.
(He doesn't like them any more than she does.)

The Penis of a Large Horse

The only penis she had ever seen
before the night she saw her late husband's
(who wasn't 'late' then, by the way)
was the penis of a large horse.
It dangled in the sun among the buttercups
as if it shared the coos and neighs of summer.

The Top of the Hill

Sometimes she will find herself in bed
still fully dressed, even with her sandals on;
at other times she'll find herself downstairs
receiving guests in a threadbare nightgown;
today she wears a sensible headscarf
for striding to the top of the hill.

Mother

Mother said *It's dog eat dog out there!*
Men will come and peel back your skin.
Well, Vera longed to feel *peeled back*.
To be so wrecked she couldn't even breathe!
But did she want a husband? She did not.
Who needs husbands cluttering up the place?
She needs to *get ahead* and other people
can go and get ahead *somewhere else!*...
Now Vera's much too sick to get ahead.
She's never felt so sick! *It serves her right.*
The old are old, Vera. It's impossible
not to be, at your age, dear. Get used to it.

Lola

Lola's peering down at Vera's hair.
She pokes it with the 'wrong' end of the comb.
(Part of her, the nasty little part,
is envious of Lola and her combs.)

The Sponge Cake

In order to perfect her look, a hat,
a raspberry-coloured hat, has appeared –
the icing on the cake, as it were.
A fluffy sponge cake with a deadly filling.

The Ambulance

He's waffling on to someone she can't see
and now the little dogs begin their yapping,
nowadays dogs are yapping everywhere,
why can't people have a silent pet?
She settles on her balcony and watches him
and wonders if he knows how bald he is...
Suddenly an ambulance shrieks past,
he waves at her as if he thinks it's fun,
as if he thinks they're friends, which they aren't,
she can do without friends like him,
the friends that Vera wants are *cultured friends*,
a cultured man whose only pets are fish.

The Tennis Dress

She stuffs a bristly leg into a stocking
and listens to the moths as they hurl themselves
from side to side against the wobbling lampshade.
The fact that she was once a trampolinist
sixty years ago is not the point.
Nor the fact that once upon a time
everyone agreed he was handsome.
The old are old, Vera dear. Get used to it.
Vera has got whiskers on her chin.
She yanks them out with tweezers. Her old neck
always looks grimy for some reason.
(It's easy to look grimy when you're old!)
She brushes her elasticated trousers.
(Her waist was last measured for a tennis dress!)
Her neighbour leaves the house in tiny shorts,
waving to astonished girls and women.
He used to fly light aircraft for moguls
who knew he was a man they could trust.

The Pearl Necklace

No amount of jewels will prevent
the horse-like face from looking bad-tempered,
in spite of being born a millionairess.
In spite of or *because of*. After all,
being born wasn't her fault.
A millionairess is a millionairess.

The Lagonda

The hairdresser is getting her a drink.
Someone else helps her to a chair.
The long-haired vicar asks her how she is
then scoots away to sit beside the nieces.
The merriment begins! But where is Vera?
A nice young man has given her a lift,
right to her front door, in his Lagonda.

The Question

If he were to reappear, they asked her,
would she have him back, is the question.
Stupid question! Won't even go there!
It's Vera, on the contrary, who is risen.
Risen like the Lord, or a cake.

The Smell of Cows

Everywhere she goes she smells cows.
Even the montbretia smells of cows.
She's sitting on a hillside on the bench
in memory of someone who enjoyed
not only cows but also sitting down.
She'll be fine once she's sitting down.
The smell of cows plus sitting down: perfect!
Vera understands the smell of cows.

Crying for No Reason

He couldn't stand the way Vera *fussed*,
the way she'd spend all morning in the bathroom
crying *for no reason*. Now, of course,
she can cry all day if she wants to.
She sinks into a chair. (On the radio
a man explains a gnu is an antelope.)
She reaches for a chocolate crème and shoves it,
and another, down her fat throat.
The nextdoor neighbour's hair-do is so big
it really needs a bungalow of its own!
(It's not an ox and not a buffalo.)
Vera hears the non-existent antelope
serenely chewing non-existent flowers
and on her chubby fingers she can feel
the non-existent warmth of his breath.

The Sultan's Fragrant Concubines

The nextdoor neighbour's dragging out his bin.
His hands are getting more and more misshapen.
Where do robins go when it's dark?
She'll give him some sultanas in the morning.
(Him, the *robin*, not the nextdoor neighbour.
Sultanas, not the sultan's fragrant concubines.)
She keeps forgetting everyone has died.
That she is now the matriarch of *nothing*.
Never mind. She shuffles to the bathroom.
Her nightie is so fluffy it's like lint.
(Lint or *sin*. Sin is fluffy too.)

Truffles

Yesterday she didn't trust the doctor,
today she doesn't trust her own solicitor,
tomorrow she will trust everyone.
More than trust. Shower them with truffles
that they can only gawp at and decline.

Yellow Ducks

She's sitting in the bathroom on the chair
on which she sits to expiate her sins,
how long she has been sitting here who knows
(or what *to sin*, or *expiation*, means)
or not so much expiate as *dwell on*,
and not so much her own as other people's.
Her husband's, for example. Now he's 'passed'
she lets herself dwell on them in peace,
while peeping through the greeny-grey curtains,
the sort of scented, greeny-grey curtains
that dying people hide behind to die,
they bob along like faded rubber ducks
bobbing in a bathtub, then they die.
(Her husband got that same sickly yellow,
and more and more chilly to the touch,
and then – or was it earlier – he died.)
Here he comes, the neighbour, he looks up
and then pretends he didn't look up.

The Leotard

One of Vera's breasts is hanging out!
(She didn't seem to care, he tells us later,
either that or else she didn't know.
He also says she gave him a leotard.
She knew his little daughter liked ballet
and bought it specially for her, he says.
Her breast was long and thin and clearly visible.
It dangled down, he adds, like a limb.)

The New Pair of Shoes

She dreams she saws her leg off at the knee
and people come from far and wide to marvel at her –
the leg, the saw, the blood, the blood-stained shoe.
And by the morning Vera has decided
to buy herself a new pair of shoes!
The trouble is she ends up on the floor,
wriggling like an upside-down-goldfish
that can't remember where its legs should be.

The Silver Hair

Everyone must die. Fair enough.
Vera's husband, yes. But not Vera!
(Did I ever tell you how he died?
It was on the very day, apparently,
he found a silver hair on his jacket
– silver! Like the coming of the Lord!)
Vera stowed the hair in her locket.
The husband she despatched to the morgue.

What Vera Needs

Stink, stench, fetidity, whatever.
What Vera needs is *regular visitors.*
Lola will arrange for her cousin,
the one who is a cleaner, to pop in.
The plumber says it's creepy in there.
(The father of the dancer, remember?)
He says he can't explain it, it's just creepy.
Well, if he can't explain it – *shut up!*
So Vera stinks. Well, Lola doesn't mind:
it's possible to stink and still be human.

Arboriculture

Does Vera really talk to him? She does.
Not *out loud* obviously, but still...
Little things like how his tree is doing.
And if she gets a bit upset sometimes
he always says *Vera, you will love it!*
Always in that reassuring tone.

Froth

Large and fragrant (like a launderette
that smells of bedding and encrusted froth,
froth that's now the texture of holly)
Vera sits and glares at the street,
at people getting younger and younger
and further and further away.

The Suitcase

Vera must have fallen asleep.
She's nestled in the old wing-back chair,
a blanket on her lap, making grunting noises.
How odd to think she has survived them all –
hubby, sisters, various small dogs,
the grumpy cat that bit the undertaker...
Her feet are resting on a leather case,
ready packed. (She's not going anywhere!)

The Lovely Nurses

She whacks the lovely nurses with her stick
and when the handsome doctor reappears
she screams at him she *wishes he was dead!*
She rages like a star that's been abandoned
in outer space for billions of years...
for billions of years she has been searching
for somewhere she will recognise as home.

Vera in the Bathroom with Her Puzzle Book

Vera's sitting quietly with her puzzle book
wrapped in an enormous fluffy towel.
Can she find a word with 5 consonants
and only one vowel? Yes she can!
Easy one! *Warmth* is the answer.

DRESSED AND SOBBING

Woman on a Sofa

I did my best
but he was never satisfied,
he trembled
with a sort of constant rage,
he'd hit the roof
if he could see me now,
my shoes all wet
and dog-hairs in my pudding.

Orange Juice

I'm shuffling to the bathroom in my dressing-gown
when suddenly I help myself to orange juice,
far too much,
why do I keep doing that,
gulping mugs of juice
for no reason
at dead of night
when all the owls are watching,
replete with mouse-blood,
from their mighty oaks,
mouse-blood,
there's no way I'm drinking mouse-blood.

Large and Small and Medium-sized Facecloths

Everybody had to have their facecloth bag
to keep their facecloth in
to take back home,
the bags were large and pink
and not unlike
the breasts that keep on getting in my way,
I see they can't be bothered any more
to even have the decency to duck.

The Woman in the Bathroom Mirror

I thought the old had always been that way,
had never been first young
and then old,
until I saw my face
like a foot
scowling at me from the bathroom mirror.

What's That Hand Doing in My Sock

When I saw the hand I thought
Hello
What's that hand doing in my sock
and then it stopped
and seemed to wave at me,
a speckled hand that could have been my mother's
but no, the hand was mine,
or was it mine,
what if no one's there
where the me
that is or isn't me
isn't hiding,
maybe I'm not here and the hand
works alone,
rearranging socks,
scratching pigs' ears, for example,
maybe there is no one here to hear
the grunts of pigs transported into Paradise.

A Grandmother in Jeans

When I saw her,
dressed in skin-tight jeans,
a floral blouse, a gold plastic belt,
teetering down the high street in front of me,
a voice inside me shouted *Please no*,
can't she understand
it's gross
at her age
to go about in jeans
but *oh dear*
I'm wearing jeans myself,
and I'm much older,
I seem to think I'm somehow exempt,
not think exactly,
I assume I am,
I'm like the man who says he's the Messiah,
he can wear whatever he wants,
a robe, a wreath, a pair of sturdy sandals,
maybe a gold watch with flashing beeps.

The Pianist

Two seagulls have arrived on my roof
as if to say it isn't 'my roof' anyway,
as if I should be honoured,
and I am,
I like to hear them crashing on my roof,
do they know how old I am,
they don't,
how old and fat,
they neither know nor care,
I like the way they boldly take up residence
above my head
as if I'm not there,
I like their tiny knees,
their flat feet,
I like the way they suddenly head off,
their wings like hands
outstretched
across a keyboard,
my brother's hands,
which seemed so bold and white,
I'd watch them as he sat at the piano,
his back to me,
I could forget the face
and having to be seen by the face
and having to arrange what it would see.

Women in Blankets

People younger people call their *loved* ones,
people who are, sometimes if not always,
easier to love if they're dead,
or young again,
one or the other,
who mutter,
who disown their arms and legs,
people wrapped in grey-green greasy blankets,
these are now my people,
now I'm older,
the daughter of a mother
it's too late
to say I'm sorry to
for being me,
to say I'm sorry for exhausting her.
(After I was born, he said,
she changed,
after that she *never smiled again.*)

A Story about Moose

When I see how casually she flips
first one
and then the other
floppy breast,
flips or flicks,
like flicking locks of hair,
or like my uncle
flipping his cigar-box lid,
when she pats them dry underneath
then flicks the towel
up between her legs
while telling us her story about moose,
it makes it feel fun
to have become,
without our being aware of it,
much older,
so cosy in our large expensive swimwear
designed for those who are too fat for lace.

The Visitor

Most nights
I wake up four or five times
and wander round the room
in the half-light
not knowing what to do,
I peer at stars,
I irritate the cat,
I rearrange
my underwear across the heated towel-rail,
it was on already when I came,
silent, warm, contented,
like a cow
that only ever wants to be a cow,
and if and when they're moody,
and they can be,
I won't name names,
but one in particular
(the gloom and doom,
the sighs,
the long face
that looks at me as if I'm just a flickering
guest-house television turned to mute)
I stroke my heated towel-rail
and I tell myself
how good it feels to feel so fond of it,
how careful I must be not to hurt him,
that's the last thing I would want to do.

Pies

Shouldn't I have learnt by now
to live with it,
isn't that the point of being old,
but no, I have to get upset again,
why can't I just *take* it
like the women
sitting in the baths with their shmice,
I don't know how to spell it,
it's what looks like
a cross between a loofah and a whip,
they sit and smile like enormous pies.

Lying on My Back in the Dark

I'm lying on my back in the dark,
there's something in my bed,
it's in my chest,
busy in my chest
like a rat
that's made its nest inside me,
in my ribs,
a rat without a face
I must obey
and *obey I will*
on pain of death.

Forgiveness

If to simply say 'I forgive him'
can be said to constitute forgiveness
then, OK, I say 'I forgive him',
and soon I'll be so old and simple-minded
I'll go around 'forgiving' everyone,
but sadly I'm not sure that it can.

Naughty Girls in Dark Woods

Now I'm at the age those women are
who live in lonely cottages in woods,
who feed on roots,
who scream,
who marry goats,
who wear the same black stockings day and night,
who never meet another human being
and if they do
they never talk, they scream,
and if they meet a naughty girl
they eat her,
I'm sorry but they do,
they can't help it.

Suitcase

You think you've seen it coming
but you haven't,
you think you know you know
but you don't,
you live as though you don't,
but you do,
can't you see the old on all sides,
careful not fall,
of course you can,
you've seen them all your life
like, say, potatoes,
suitcases,
things that can't move,
things that have no choice but to be patient,
you see them,
but to *be one yourself,*
that's something that you're going to have to think about,
to learn to have the courage to get used to,
get used to *fast,*
you're going to have to hurry,
your mother's died, you can't go home, *get over it,*
you can't quite hear what people say,
get over it,
you don't know what your number is,
get over it,
embrace
(I know at first it won't be easy)
embrace what happens when you go to bed,
when you're the one who finds she can't get up,
the one they keep upstairs
like a suitcase,
a suitcase full of things

they can't face up to
that used to be,
or seem,
completely different,
that used to be as fresh as a daisy,
as trusty as the eye of an ox,
as trusty and as *limpid*
if limpid
means the way it sounds as if it should.

Hootie

Yes, it takes all day,
but I don't mind,
I like to see how still I can sit,
to sit beside her like an elephant
(although it can be frightening,
something vast
which may or may not want to be benevolent,
and even if it does
it's still scary,
something vast,
that longs to be surrendered to,
seems to be behind us,
in attendance),
and when and if she speaks
she speaks reluctantly,
she speaks as if to speak will hold her back,
her terror like a beautiful gold egg
she steadies on a spoon,
she knows my voice,
I think she knows my voice,
but not my face,
she didn't burn the matron
and the suitcase
didn't beg to not be left behind,
she glares at me like somebody might glare
at artificial flowers they can't clean,
either can't or won't,
and when she glares
her face is like a cage full of owls.

How to Attract Men

I wheel her outside
with her tin
and roll her a thin cigarette
and while she smokes
I massage the feet
that never touch the ground,
like angels' feet,
she's now too bored
of being fed
to feed,
she prefers morphine and rollies,
I powder her white toes,
I brush her hair,
the long straight hair
I used to be so jealous of,
I knew that hair like that attracted men,
she feels for my hand in her darkness,
her fingers are like fingers made of oysters,
I tell her it's OK
but it's not,
I tell her angels never wear shoes
but probably they do when no one's looking.

The Woman on the Bus

This woman who is sitting right in front of me
spending the entire bumpy journey
picking at her scalp
in my face,
I never would have felt like this before,
before I was transformed into this person
who's not so much a person as a sack
someone's left unwanted babies in,
a sack that moves
but is devoid of light.

My Mother's Naked Body

Nobody must see her upset,
nobody must see her naked body,
nobody must see the upstairs room
where nothing can be heard except dust,
where nothing can be seen except dustsheets,
it's like a dusty pen where rare animals
are penned together for a million years,
nobody must go there, least of all
me,
her daughter,
with my beady eye,
never, if that's not too much to ask,
step inside that door,
she seems to say,
as, muffled, gagged,
expecting ridicule,
she backs behind her barricade of cake,
some of us are kind to her,
reluctantly,
and some of us can't be bothered, some of us
start 'saying things',
I'm sorry to say,
her daughters are God's way of being cruel to her,
one of them in particular,
the one with beady eyes and a biro,
what happened to the Osmiroid they gave her,
the Parker 51, the Mont Blanc,
but no, it has to be some cheap biro.

Semolina

I like it when they call me Semolina,
it says I'm warm and cosy,
and I am,
or anyway I was
when I was someone
with rosy cheeks
whose world made perfect sense,
you didn't need to poke at it
or question it
or brood about the nature of eternity
and is it like a great plain or isn't it,
is it like a plain of forgiveness
to which the old are leading us
like cattle,
the old, the old,
where are they now, the old,
they're staring at the fingers they can't use,
the useless limbs like stockings filled with arrowroot,
the sippy mugs,
the sponge cakes,
the azaleas,
(azaleas?
are they even flowers?)
crunchy and forgotten on the window sill,
that somebody once thought would bring them cheer,
once thought that bringing cheer was even possible,
or didn't dare admit
it's sometimes not.

Athletic, Chaste, Untroubled

Athletic, chaste, untroubled,
far from home,
I share my sherbet lemons
with the friend
who, sixty years later, will be strapped,
like someone's luggage,
to a wheelchair
and wheeled to a little patch of sun
by one of two
tired but clean nurses
to smoke her tiny rollie in peace.

Divorcee

With her curly hair and rosy cheeks,
luckily she didn't know she's not
(but she will do)
not, in fact, adored,
or shall we say she did and she didn't,
that Pony, the old pony, will die,
her lips will purse,
her hair will be tugged straight,
her mother will be called a *divorcee.*

Lilies

The lilies at the end of the garden
stank so much
you could smell their smell
inside the room my grandmother lay dying in,
lucky her,
she couldn't smell a thing,
a bed had been set up in the drawing-room
where I was led,
barefoot,
to say goodnight,
I said goodnight only to the pillow
and it was here that I began my search
for what was in due course to be a lover.

Howls of Laughter

When I was a child and I heard
howls of laughter coming from downstairs
I'd tiptoe out across the landing thinking
everybody's happy except me
but things don't seem to matter like that now,
I never sit on stairs in floods of tears
and chew the kittens off my angel-top,
I never even tiptoe any more.

Women in Pyjamas

If they thought we knew,
well, we didn't,
and here we are
stranded in our wheelchairs
or sunk into our sofas or our beds,
our swollen feet
the colour of tomato juice,
with no idea how or why we got here.

Violet

When someone dies,
the more there was a problem
the longer you will mourn them, apparently,
so maybe that explains
why I still 'mourn' her,
though I prefer 'think about' to 'mourn',
I never know what 'mourning' someone means
I think about her even more now,
now that I am old myself,
like she was,
and in my lifetime she was always old,
just as I was young and always would be,
my mother shrinking daily
like a violet
crystallised until it can't breathe.
Another reason could be, I suppose,
(although I find it painful to admit it)
because, now I'm so weak, I need a mother.

The Rooms Downstairs

Nobody lives up here except me
but from the rooms downstairs
I can hear
what sound like tears
being shed by strangers
and sometimes there's the sound of someone singing,
floorboards being swept,
loud hoots of laughter.

How to Float

Nothing else matters to me now,
nothing except love
and how to float
and how to take no notice of the clocks
and how to reinvent myself as somebody
who's not so much a person
as a turtle
who bobs along
doing nothing much,
a turtle whose idea of bliss is mud,
mud, sludge, anything pointless
and do I miss the clock ticks?
I do not.

Little Squeaks

I float along
like a sort of turtle
experimenting
with not hurrying,
money, fame, mean nothing to me now,
my ego,
what I'm guessing is my ego,
is making little high-pitched gasping-noises
and little squeaks,
but am I listening,
no,
it's easy not to listen when you're old,
it's easy just to not take any notice
of anything
except supplies of underwear.

Ants

They whizz about so madly
they're like bumper cars
and some brave souls have scaled a piece of toast,
they're so excited,
dashing left and right,
or maybe not,
maybe they are terrified,
maybe they are thinking *Oh my God*,
I'll never find true love
before it's over,
before some robin stabs me to death.

Cheese

I used to see my elderly father,
who as you know was quite a pompous person,
kneel by the skirting-board with cheese
and then the other day
to my astonishment
a dormouse tiptoed out between the lilies,
ran across my shoe,
then shot back in
as if to say *Now do you believe*
a perk of being old is seeing mice.

Dressed and Sobbing

Please can someone give me a lake
that I can go and jump in,
dressed and sobbing,
how can someone jump into a lake
without a lake
so please can someone give me one, a lake
suitable for someone who
loves jumping.